GAMECHANGER

The Baseball Parent's Ultimate Guide

Michael McCree

Contact Author By: michael.gamechanger@gmail.com

The purpose of the information contained in this book is to educate
parents on how to enhance the performance of youth baseball players.
Nothing contained in this book should be construed nor is intended to be
used for medical diagnosis or treatment. It should not be used in place of
the advice of your physician or other qualified health care provider.
Should you have any health care related questions, please call or see
your physician or other qualified health care provider promptly. Always
consult with your physician or other qualified health care provider before
embarking on a new treatment, diet, or fitness program.
You should never disregard medical advice or delay seeking it because of
something you have read in this book.
This book is also available in e-book format.

McCree, Michael.
Gamechanger: The Baseball Parent's Ultimate Guide/ by Michael
McCree.
Includes bibliographical references.

ISBN-10: 06 15972616
ISBN-13: 978-0-615-97261-9

1. Parenting-Sports 2. Parenting – Psychological Aspects 3. Sports-
Psychological

Editor: Laura Apperson
Interior Formatting and Design: Anna N. Yang

Book Cover Design by Leslie K. © 2014 Super Massive 3D

Printed in the United States of America

Dedication

To my mother, Carrie McCree, who
for many years went extraordinary
lengths to ensure that I was able to
participate in the game that I loved.

Special Thanks

To my former coaches who have taught me life lessons through baseball that I will carry with me for the rest of my life in all endeavors.

To clients that have trusted me with the on-going development of their sons.

Also, I would like to thank others who have helped along the way:
Allen Thomas
Patrick Wright
Mike Matheny
Laster King
Jasha Balcom
Gradey Caldwell
Joseph Batten

Table of Contents

Title Page

Foreword

For many years, I have been immensely fortunate to have the rare opportunity to enrich the lives of those who seek to make their child's experience playing baseball memorable. Although parents have expressed an outpouring of genuine gratitude for my services as a private instructor and team coach, I feel as if I owe *them*. They have given me the opportunity to give priceless knowledge and information: knowledge and information that could potentially be the gateway to a newfound self-esteem, a more enjoyable experience, a much-needed discipline, and a multitude of other benefits that the game of baseball has to offer.

Though I was involved in baseball for over twenty years, I never envisioned being a coach while I was a player. As a player, my main focus was on just that—playing. When my career was over, I was left with the decision of what I would do next with my life. After graduating from college and coming to the realization that I was done playing the game I loved so much, I had to figure out how I would make a living in the real world. Apprehensive, somewhat reluctant, and in need of some form of income, I accepted a job to privately instruct young baseball players at a local indoor facility. This is where I would begin to teach the basics of the game. Little did I know that this experience would change my life. Business was slow in the beginning and thoughts of getting a "real job" circled frequently in my mind. Over time, I was given the opportunity to work with more and more players on a consistent basis as I built up my clientele. Through working consistently with young men who were on the same journey that I once was, I had developed a heartfelt desire to deliver the highest quality of service to each and every player imaginable. It became my obligation to provide them with all the knowledge I wish I had received on my quest for success on the field.

Over the years, parents have—with unnecessary shame—admitted to a lack of knowledge when it comes to specifics of the game. Since I am trusted with the assignment of enhancing their child's performance, I listen to a variety of concerns from parents. I get a firsthand account of some of the questions that all parents have in the baseball community when it comes to on- and off-the-field matters.

Being the "middle man" for a child's growth and success helped me realize the wonderful opportunity I had been given. I found myself graciously giving priceless bits of information to baseball players, coaches, moms, and dads (and in some cases, grandparents).

In this book, I will share information on various topics pertaining to specific questions and concerns that parents raising baseball players may have. This information is meant solely to empower the baseball parents and make them aware of the vital role they play in this process of success on the playing field.

With a combination of playing and coaching experience, I have been able to "connect the dots" *and* analyze aspects of baseball that I wish I would have paid more attention to as a player. The old adage "If I knew what I know now…" is a very fitting expression. Looking back on the past and realizing the necessity of this vital information, I have realized how much I need to share my knowledge and experiences.

This book was written with the purpose of enlightening parents to the fact that they too—regardless of athletic background or know-how—can effectively impact the performance of their beloved child in a positive fashion. The information that I will share is only intended to provoke constructive thoughts that may have never been considered. I assure you that you will be far more knowledgeable on select topics related to youth baseball upon the completion of this material. This project is simply a labor of love, created from the bottom of my heart as a token of my appreciation for the game of baseball and all that it has done for me.

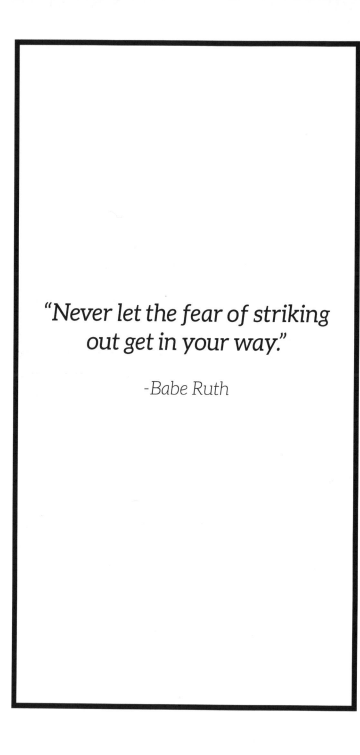

"Never let the fear of striking out get in your way."

-Babe Ruth

Introduction

Baseball: \\'bās-ˌbol\ *a bat-and-ball sport played between 2 teams of 9 players each. The aim is to score runs by hitting a thrown ball with a bat and touching a series of four bases arranged at the courses of a 90-foot diamond.**

Although there is a general consensus that the game of baseball was invented and originated in Europe, the sole person responsible for the idea is currently unknown. Nevertheless, whoever it was most certainly did not anticipate the magnitude at which this game would have an impact on the world and the millions who would later associate with it throughout history. It is incredible to think that the world could be impacted by a person who was perhaps stricken with boredom to the point where they decided to create a game with a ball and a stick. Whoever it was in the 1800s that invented it certainly did not live to see it evolve over the centuries into the national pastime that it is in the United States and the beloved sport that is played professionally across the globe.

Baseball is perhaps one of the most-played sports among youth athletes in America and even in other parts of the world. It is arguably one of the easiest games to conceptualize, and the majority of people understand the main premise and objective of the game. For every child playing on a baseball diamond, there are—in most cases—two parents with the responsibility of picking up, dropping off, buying equipment; and cheering in the rain, sleet, snow, spring, the dead heat of summer, fall, and sometimes winter. They also have the parental duties of giving advice, regardless if the advice is qualified or not.

Although parents aren't the ones running bases, diving for balls, or swinging at pitches from the opposing team, they *feel* just as much a part of the game as if they were tying up their cleats and hitting the field themselves. A parent feels the psychological ups and downs the player experiences. Although the parents may not know the specifics of the game, they are fully aware of the psychological roller coaster ride on which this game can take someone. So, why do we love the game so much? Well, you could ask 100 people why and you may get 100 different answers.

From diving catches in the outfield to 6-4-3 double plays to game-winning homeruns, we could all come up with a million and one reasons to love baseball. It is easy to think of our own reasons, but to pinpoint someone else's reasons as to why they love the game so much may offer a challenge. For parents, this means considering why your child may love the game. If you're reading this book, you have an interest in how to effectively influence. Influencing meaningfully entails having a thorough knowledge of who you are attempting to influence. So, why do young men of youth age love the game of baseball so much? The answer may be rather simple: it's a **game**.

Does this sound like an answer that is far too simplistic to take seriously? It is very simplistic. Most individuals tend to lose sight of this. We get caught up in all the hoopla, competition, and emotion that cloud our minds and divert it from the real premise.

Although the discipline, hard-work, sportsmanship, perseverance, and other aspects of personal development are extremely important, having fun with the game makes all of these efforts worthwhile. We often lose sight of the fact that in games, we seek to have fun. However, parents can unknowingly alter the circumstances and create a dynamic that can cause for a less-than-desirable experience. Teaching you how to be a parent is definitely not the objective of this book. If you're traveling across state lines and spending valuable time, energy, money and countless resources to ensure your child gets to play out on the field, you obviously have much love and passion for your child's success.

Oftentimes, this passion can just be misdirected. I hope that in sharing this information, you will consider aspects of your journey with your child that you may have never thought about previously. As the great saying goes, "Knowledge is power."

If used effectively, the knowledge expressed within these lessons will provide you with a sense of power as you handle vital circumstances during your child's baseball career.

"Little League baseball is a very good thing because it keeps the parents off the streets."

-Yogi Berra

1

Character Building in Baseball

Main reasons that parents sign their children up for baseball:

1. Extracurricular activity.
2. Intentions of playing at a higher level in the future.
3. Life lessons that baseball is capable of teaching.

Perhaps you may have never thought of the reasons why you signed your son up until now. You may identify yourself as a parent who has gotten your ball player involved for one or two of the reasons listed above. A select few of you may have chosen the involvement for not just all three reasons, but for others that aren't included.

If you haven't thought about it prior to owning this book, I would like you to take a minute or two to think about it. Knowing can help you figure out what positive attributes and benefits youth baseball can provide. If you were once unaware of the beneficial life lessons that baseball can offer, hopefully this information will make you aware of its character-building abilities.

How Baseball Can Build Character

Every sport has the ability to build character in some way. Each of them can offer opportunities to learn and grow from a discipline and a work ethic standpoint. Baseball is very unique in its own right when it comes to character-building. Not only does it build character but it is also the ultimate tool to *expose* character. It's a great tool for gauging levels of self-discipline, mental toughness, team-player skills, perseverance, and more.

Many players, as well as parents around the world, are sometimes unaware of the long-term life skills that can be cultivated and lessons that can be learned if the game is approached from a more conscientious perspective. Baseball being a "skill sport" doesn't mean automatic success for the physically gifted athlete. Being strong, fast, or tall in stature has never made a player a "shoe in" at being successful. Although these are great attributes for anyone to possess, it doesn't always equate to being a great player.

Baseball teaches you to not only analyze your opponent but it also teaches you that before you can study your opponent, you must fully know yourself and where you are as a player. For example, it would do little good to have figured out when, what, and how an opposing pitcher was throwing his pitches to me if I did not have my swing right in such a way that would allow me to capitalize on the knowledge I gained about his pitching tendencies. Of course you should know what your opponent may be intending to do, but not at the expense of knowing the depths of your own strengths and weaknesses first.

Sacrifice

Baseball teaches sacrifice. Each sport has its own elements of sacrifice on an individual and/or team level. In basketball, players risk bodily harm by taking charges in attempts to draw offensive fouls on the other team. In football, players have to be very physical in order to block opponents as a means of helping their teammates make it to the end zone. Baseball is unique in the way that a sacrifice for the team could cause a lowering of statistical data that reflects personal performance.

For example, a sacrifice *pop fly* to move a runner ahead or a purposely hit groundball to help a teammate advance into scoring position could negatively affect a player's numerical stats. It's easy to sacrifice when there isn't as much on the line, as in other sports, which is why baseball is an ultimate teacher of sacrifice. Where else would you find a player willing to stand in place while a hard, round object came barreling in his direction and, although having the option of moving out of the way, decides to stand there and "take one for the team" in order to reach first base on a "hit by pitch?"

Perseverance

Learning to cultivate a spirit of perseverance is a meaningful lesson in baseball. This is especially true since players sometimes go through long stretches of time where they may not be playing up to their personal standards. Opportunities to make up for errors and mistakes may take longer than other sports. For example, in the game of basketball, a player may miss an easy, close-range jump shot; however, he is able to make up for it rather quickly by making a good play on defense. This can be the same with football, since both of these sports have a more fast-paced tempo.

In baseball, a player can strike out with teammates in scoring position (standing on second or third base) for the last out of the inning. In this case, there is no chance for immediate redemption. He will either have to wait for the team to cycle through the batting order until it is his turn to hit again, or, in other cases, he'll have to wait until the *next* game to get a chance to make up for a letdown.

As a player, I remember this being a very frustrating feeling. Being eager to get back in the game and to get another shot at redeeming myself was all I could think about. Knowing that you'd have to wait for that one opportunity to redeem yourself is sure to cause anxiety. This element of the game requires a lot of mental toughness.

Focusing on what you can control

In baseball, focusing only on what you can control is essential to keeping a calm demeanor. In a sport like football, size can be a major contributor in the differentiation of two players, which ultimately affects the outcome. However, since baseball is not a contact sport, an opponent's physical stature should not cause worry. This is something that still concerns many young players when they see opponents who may be bigger in size.

As a baseball player, it is extremely important to stay

focused on doing your job in one single moment. For example, I like to tell clients of mine that "a ground ball is a ground ball" or "a pop fly is a pop fly." This simply means that regardless of whose bat the ball came off, it is up to you to do what's necessary to field a ground ball properly or to catch a fly ball. Regardless of the pitcher, it is your duty to swing at a good pitch. A player with this type of approach to the game will not be affected by the physical stature of opponents.

In these messages that I teach my players, it reinforces the belief that their achievement is solely based on them. This is the message we must send to our youth players. The character-building lessons of the game can serve an individual well. Many of the lessons are learned consciously and some are learned unconsciously. Parents, if well aware, can help a player get the most out of every experience of the game from a character-building point of view.

"*People ask me what I do in winter when there's no baseball. I'll tell you what I do. I stare out the window and wait for spring.*"

-Rogers Hornsby

2

Pre-game Conversations

Parent-to-child talks are a majorly important part of the success of an impressionable young man who seeks advice in any sport. Your son is a sponge, ready to soak up much-needed counseling from his mother or father. With this in mind, understand that your every word could prove crucial in your son's outlook on any situation.

The game of baseball, being a mental warzone at times, is a game that requires a cool, calm, and collected demeanor. Knowing this should awaken a certain level of heightened awareness in your choice of words to your son before a game. Living vicariously through your son can be detrimental if it puts unnecessary stress on you, and even more so if it carries over to your son, who strives to please you. Here are a few tips that will keep you on the right track when giving constructive pre-game pep talks:

1. Create a relaxed environment with the goal of having fun

The number one reason kids love to play baseball isn't for the cool uniform or because it gets their heart rates up for good exercise. Kids love to play baseball because it is FUN! Take away the fun in baseball and the experience turns into a waste of hours running around in dirt while they could have been doing something else more fun (not to mention a waste of *your* time and money). This is the main thing you want to stress to your son. After all, athletes who have more fun while competing give more effort.

2. Don't be too talkative

Talking too much or bringing up unnecessary points will most likely cause nervousness or agitation. Remember, the more you say, the more your son absorbs. The last thing you want to do is create emotional or psychological exhaustion before a competitive game. When giving your positive advice, be "short and sweet." Getting to the point of the discussion can prevent the conversation from going into left field (no pun intended), beyond your original intentions of the initial conversation.

3. Don't sound threatening

Regardless of previous performance on the field, it is important to avoid a dictator-like attitude towards your son. Intimidating a player into having a good game is not the answer. If they have been struggling at the plate or have had trouble in the field, remind them that this could be the game to turn it all around. This will create an opportunity that will entice a player to *want* to redeem himself from past poor performances.

4. Give goals to attain

Having a game plan is essential in the mental aspect of the game of baseball. Putting focus on one or two aspects of the game can "quiet" the mind and help to reduce anxiety. Make it a habit to speak about setting small, attainable goals before games. Goals should be set that are specific for that particular game.

For example, a simple goal could be for the player to get on base at least twice in the upcoming game through either a hit or a base on balls. Another example could be that a pitcher's goal is to give up no more than three walks during the innings he pitches in that particular game.

Imagination and the Power of Positive Thinking

These talks can provide an opportunity for the parent to lead in the imagination process. If done right, the parent can guide a player through the uncharted, never-visited areas of his mind, helping him discover the power of imagination and visualizing success before it is realized in actuality. Imagination can be used as a means of helping a player not just think, but actually *feel* what type of results he wants in the upcoming game.

Pre-game talks from a parental figure will often carry the undertone of *expectation*. The discussion of a player's success when coming from a parent will most certainly always come from a place that is indicative of the level of expectations they have of that particular player. This is why it is essential to take a conscious look at how a parent is formulating their expectations of their ballplayer, as mentioned previously.

"There are three types of baseball players: Those who make it happen, those who watch it happen and those who wonder what happens."

-Tommy Lasorda

3

Managing Expectations

There have been many debates, arguments, and studies surrounding parent-child relationships as it pertains to expectations. Should the parent(s) set high expectations for their children with the possibility of them being let down when they don't live up to what's expected? Or should parents be lenient when setting expectations for the children to help them feel more accomplished?

I always find it best for parents to set high yet realistic goals for their player. Setting high, achievable goals will give players the opportunity to do what is necessary to increase their *own* standards. When the child knows much is expected of them from the parent, the need to impress and satisfy will increase the desire to strive and reach those heights. Yet reasonable goals leave room for kids to still be kids.

Not setting goals that will push the player to work harder will make mediocrity acceptable, which may cause complacency.

Let's use weightlifting as an example. If you walk into the gym with the expectation that the most you can lift on bench press is 100 pounds, chances are you will not attempt to lift beyond that amount for fear that you will fail and perhaps drop the weight on your chest. However, if your muscles are in fact able to lift 150 pounds, and you only lift 100 pounds, you are doing the muscles no good because you are not exercising them to their potential.

If in this situation we continue on the path of not lifting that of which we are capable, we will never become strong enough to increase our muscular strength so that we can lift more. This represents how low expectations and fear of failure can contribute to little or no progress.

Parents must be very clear with their expectations. Being firm with "non-negotiables" is a must.

"Non-negotiables" may include things like:
- *Playing hard*
- *Good sportsmanship*
- *Hustling on and off the field*
- *Respecting coaches, parents, and teammates*

These "non-negotiables" should be a mandated standard.

Expectations that are strictly performance based may include:
- *Making the All-Star team*
- *Number of strikeouts on the mound*
- *Number of hits*
- *Fielding Percentage*
- *Other numerical statistics*

These performance-based expectations are all tangibles with which most are familiar. These types of expectations are easily trackable because there is evidence to show for them after a game. However, the intangible expectations that every player should have of *himself* is of the utmost importance. These are somewhat similar to the "non-negotiable" expectations referred to earlier. The only difference is that these intangible self-expectations can't be monitored or "kept in check." Every player (the ones who take themselves seriously and intend to progress) should have a self-regulated list of *"have-to's"*:

- *I have to pay full attention to constructive criticism.*
- *I have to improve on the things today that I struggled with yesterday at practice.*
- *I have to compete at a higher level than my competition.*
- *I have to maintain good body language during practice and games.*

These are just a few mild examples of a host of expectations to which a player should hold himself. These are things that a parent can help instill from early on.

An unbearable level of expectations can be very discouraging to a young player, so it is always important to at least be aware of the things that are said in reference to a player's game play. Oftentimes a player will forecast or predict the outcome of a bad game while envisioning the turmoil of what the ride home is going to be like if they happen to not play well.

This is normally due to the child being conditioned by the type of treatment they normally receive from the parent following a particular type of performance. Your son will undoubtedly pick up subtle and not-so-subtle signals from you about how you feel through what they feel you are thinking, by what they hear you saying or by what they see you doing.

As a parent, it is important to make sure that the player knows that their expectations of themselves should always be higher priority than the parent's expectations of them. The players are the ones playing the game, and should want to strive to do their best.

This notion will get them in tune with their internal drive and their inner motivation to do well for *themselves*. Of course, as the parent, you will relay your expectations to them, but it's important they know that these set of expectations are different. Many times expectations from parents get skewed when they are coupled with unhealthy comparisons.

"Every day is a new opportunity. You can build on yesterday's success or put its failures behind and start over again. That's the way life is, with a new game every day, and that's the way baseball is."

-Bob Feller

4

Comparisonitis

Over the years I've exchanged information and ideas to parents who suffer from something I like to call "comparisonitis." I use this term to describe parents who fret and worry when it comes to how other kids are performing in relation to how *their* child is performing. It is natural to compare the success of those of the same age group and level.

We have to change our perception of how we compare particular baseball players to their peers, especially at younger age groups. Parents often feel a slight sense of pressure for their sons when they see others on his team or around his league who are performing at a higher level.

"Michael, I just don't get it. Some of Tommy's teammates are hitting the ball deep into the outfield. They seem to have much more power than he does and that's a concern for me! I wish he was able to knock some balls out their over the heads of the outfielders the way some of the

big hitters on his team do, but all we've been experiencing lately is groundball after groundball in the infield. I've tried getting him to swing harder and to put more lift on the ball to try and generate some more power. I just don't know what to do to help him now."

Like I mentioned, it's very understandable that, as a parent, you will sometimes unconsciously make these comparisons. While sports bring out the inner competitor in us all, we would be foolish to think that it wouldn't also affect us in this situation. What has to be realized is that each player's growth and development will differ, especially in the younger age groups. Growth spurts are going to happen at different rates for each individual. This is generally common knowledge, but this often tends to be forgotten in a competitive environment.

In my playing days, being the team leader in certain categories frequently crossed my mind. Witnessing a teammate (or an opposing player) make diving plays, strike batters out, or crush balls off the centerfield wall always got my competitive juices flowing. Who doesn't want the adoration of the coaches and fans who come to watch you play? This is not something that is out of the ordinary; however, we must keep things in perspective. Baseball is a game that is constantly played with the notion that you are playing against *yourself.* Once a player realizes that he is ultimately in an endless race to outperform his "self of yesterday," he will reach a new level of understanding and his approach to the game will reflect that understanding.

"No one in the entire world can do a better job of being you than you."

Competing vs. Comparing

Players who focus on their own individualistic goals and tasks tend to devote themselves only to the aspects of the game over which they have control. Young ball players must be taught at a very early age that *competing* does not equate to *comparing*.

When comparing ourselves to others, rarely do we reflect on how much better we are than them; rather, we are usually analyzing the ways the other person is better than *us*. While reviewing shortcomings in a skillful manner is good for any player who intends to elevate to the next level, doing it in this fashion will kill spirits by diminishing self-worth and value in one's own mind. This can plant an undeniable seed of doubt and feeling of inadequacy that can lead to poor performances. A heavy dose of unhealthy comparisons can lead to a development of insecurities that may cause what is called **confirmation bias**.

Confirmation bias is the tendency of individuals to favor evidence that will confirm their preconceived beliefs. This type of dynamic can prove to be detrimental if a player is experiencing low self-esteem. Comparing his physical stature, muscle build, statistics, or any other attribute can serve as a means of confirming negative thoughts he already has of himself.

Since not all players are created equal, take time to explain the concept of each player bringing something different to the table of competition. After all, this is what creates the excitement of the game. The wide spectrum and variation of talent levels is what contributes to the enjoyment of the competition that the game of baseball has to offer.

"In baseball, you can't kill the clock. You've got to give the other man his chance. That's why this is the greatest game."

-Earl Weaver

5

Finding a Role on the Team

In order to boost self-esteem and self-image, make sure that your child understands the role that he plays on the team. Naturally, we all would like to believe our child should be the star on every team they play on from tee-ball and beyond. This is nothing to feel bad about since you want to see them at their very best. However, a miscalculation of proper expectations is a recipe for disappointment.

The main goal is to help them understand what their niche is and focus in on it. Be wise and take a good look at their best assets and what special contribution they make to the team.

In order to be completely committed and have a sense of purpose in anything, we have to feel that what we do has a sense of meaning. Playing on a team and feeling that you don't have a specific part in the success can become a very dull experience and can be very discouraging. This means that it's a must for a player to value the unique things that they bring to the table.

They must be reminded of their *strengths* and understand the importance they offer. If you have a ball player blessed with a sufficient amount of skill in multiple areas, that's an advantage. However, not everyone is born as talented as others and may only be able to display one or two clearly defined skills.

In this case, it is the parent's duty to make the player aware of this skill. These could include speed, good hands for fielding, an above average throwing arm, great hand-eye coordination, team leadership, or hitting power. There are many other positive qualities a player could have.

Some parents feel it may be somewhat difficult to point out one specific feature in their player, but this is when we take the time to think hard about it and find out. No one quality may jump out at you right away, but with a little reflection, it can be done.

Once this is identified, be sure to include this bit of information during pre-game and post-game discussions. This will give them the focused attention that is needed to concentrate on one particular outcome as opposed to being overwhelmed by the pressure to perform beyond their capabilities. If you're up-to-date on the latest "niche players" in the Major Leagues, be sure to use examples of other players that are similar to them that they can look up to and model their game after.

A good example of this could be that your hometown Major League team has a pinch hitter or platoon player who has recently been performing fairly well off the bench or during certain game situations as a substitute. This would be an excellent way to show your child that even players at the highest level of the game are recognized for playing their designated roles to the best of their abilities.

Here is an example:

> *Johnny, nine years old, has been struggling at the plate with his hitting. This has really taken a toll on his self-esteem because it seems as if everyone else on the team has been playing tremendously well. This forces Johnny to feel that he has not been able to contribute to the team's recent achievements. After much consideration and reflection, Johnny's father notices that he's been still getting on base by getting walks. Johnny's father reminds him that in order for the team to have success, they need players to get on base to score runs. He makes Johnny aware that with his patience at the plate, this allows for other hitters to score him in, resulting in more and more runs for the team.*

This is just one of many examples that could be used as an opportunity to remind a ball player of a significant role they play. They often attempt to compete with teammates who accomplish what others would deem to be a bigger contribution to the team. Being caught up in the glitz and glamour of the homeruns that someone else on the team hits may put unneeded pressure on him.

It is important to teach players to take pride in whatever they do best. This can be achieved by praising that which they do best. It is unlikely that most other parents on the team will congratulate your player for his specific team role, simply because they aren't thinking about the game on a deeper level, which is not something of which *you* have control. If the praise and encouragement is not coming from the outside, then it certainly needs to come from the inner circle, which is you—the parent.

Your son may not always play the position you would like him to play, hit in the batter order, or pitch in the rotation you see fit. Regardless of where or in what capacity a player is asked to help the team, he must always do the best he can in *that* particular area. Besides his defensive position, the batting order of a team line-up tends to be one of the most controversial. Despite being placed in a line-up position that may be considered undesirable by the player and/or parent, there is always an opportunity to play well for the team.

Here is a synopsis of the duties of each player within the average baseball line-up:

First Hitter—"Leadoff man:"

The leadoff man in the hitting order is, by default, a unique position. He is the first hitter of the game for his team and has an opportunity to set the tone for the rest of the game. The leadoff man is not usually known for his power as a hitter, but more so for speed and ability to reach base, which will allow him to score off of the hit from a player hitting in the line-up after him. Leadoff hitters usually have the following characteristics:

- Above-average running speed and quickness.
- Ability to make contact with the ball and are difficult to strike out.
- Patient and willing to wait on a good pitch to hit or take a walk (**base on balls**) when he doesn't receive a good pitch.

Second Hitter—"The Table Setter:"

The second hitter in the lineup is a very important part of the batting order as well. His job is normally to get on base for the third, fourth, and fifth hitter to be batted in. However, if he doesn't get on base, his next best accomplishment would be to advance the leadoff man on the bases. This would give him a chance to be batted in by the upcoming hitters in the line-up. The second hitter, in a sense, becomes the leadoff hitter if the leadoff hitter does not reach base. He usually possesses the following characteristics:

- Willing to sacrifice bunt to advance the leadoff man.
- Waits for a good pitch to hit. This can also commonly be known as having good "pitch selection."

Third, Fourth & Fifth Hitters—"The Sluggers:"

These three hitters are known to bring the "power" within the lineup. At younger age groups, this might not necessarily involve hitting homeruns but being able to hit gap-to-gap (baseballs hit deep into the outfield or to the fence). The third through fifth hitters in the order are also known to some as the "meat of the order," signifying the importance of this sector of the lineup to the success of the team offensively. Each hitter in this portion of the lineup possesses similar characteristics, yet has specific duties as well:

Third hitter— Known as the best hitter on the team. This is a player who should be able to hit for both power *and* average. This hitter is expected to have one of the highest RBI totals on the team due to scoring the leadoff and the second hitter.

Fourth hitter—Known as the "cleanup hitter," the fourth hitter is usually known as the player on the team with the most amount of hitting power. His main job is to hit for power to drive in runs.

Fifth hitter—Known as the "protector of the cleanup hitter," the fifth hitter can hit for average and power. Since teams like to "pitch around" the fourth hitter (intentionally throw out of the reach of the hitter so that he is not able to get a solid hit), the fifth hitter in the lineup must convince the opposing team he is not an easy out. Having a fifth hitter who can hit for average and power will make the opposing team think twice about intentionally letting the fourth hitter reach base with the assumption of being able to easily get the next guy out.

Sixth, Seventh and Eighth Hitters—"The bottom of the line-up."

This portion of the lineup determines the team's *true* strengths. If you want to know how strong a team is in their offense, it is usually indicative of how well the bottom of the order can perform. Even though the roles in this part of the lineup are not as specific as one through five, the bottom of the order usually consist of miscellaneous "spot duties." The job at hand will change depending on the specific game situations.

Ninth Hitter—"Second Leadoff Man."

The last hitter (oftentimes in youth baseball this could be tenth or eleventh batter depending on league rules) is often looked upon as the weakest hitter on the team. Historically, youth coaches have put the weaker hitters at the bottom of the order.

Strategically speaking, if you have two players who are candidates to be the leadoff man, a coach will decide to put one of them at the last spot in the order to serve as a "second leadoff man." Ninth hitters are especially important after the game starts and the lineup starts rotating throughout the game.

Pitcher Roles

There are three categories in which a pitcher can fit into: starter, reliever, and closer.

Starter: This pitcher is generally asked to carry much of the load on the pitching staff. It's every coach's objective to have their starting pitcher go as deep into the game as possible, lasting as many innings as they can without getting fatigued or losing control of pitches. Depending on league regulations, pitch count limits set by parents/coaches, or performance in a game, a good outing for a starting pitcher could last between a solid three to five innings.

Reliever: This pitcher is generally used immediately after a starting pitcher has come out of the game. The name says it all; they *relieve* their team of what might be a stressful situation. Need for relief could include a tired starting pitcher, a pitcher that may be out of control and throwing too many balls that are not strikes, or a coach wanting to save a pitcher's arm (save on wear and tear).

Relief pitchers can also be known as "spot pitchers," entering the game during certain situations that may yield a change of pace or a pitcher-hitter matchup. This could be when a coach recognizes a crucial moment in the game where the opponent has a left-handed hitter coming to the plate. This would call for him to bring in a left-handed pitcher in that particular moment to increase the chances of getting an out (as it has been statistically proven that it is harder to get a hit in righty vs. righty and lefty vs. lefty pitcher-hitter match-ups.)

Closer: A closing pitcher, more frequently labeled as "the closer," is a relief pitcher that specializes in getting the final outs in a game when his team is winning by a small margin. The closer is commonly known as the best reliever on the pitching staff. Since most closers are usually needed to pitch only one inning per game, it is not unusual for a closer to pitch multiple days in a row. The closer must have an attitude that will allow him to withstand the pressure of being trusted to deliver for his team in a close game. In some instances, he may enter a game where the opposing team already has runners on base threatening to score and take the lead over his team. Many within the baseball community would describe a closer as a player who needs to have "nerves of steel."

The things that most interest players are the things that provide good exercise for their abilities. On the other hand, the things that cause them to lose interest in any endeavor are the things that are beyond their abilities or are much below their abilities. This explains why it is good to have a thorough knowledge of one's role as an individual. A player knowing what his role is definitely goes hand-in-hand with how he manages expectations and comparisons. A player knowing his role will have an influence on what he expects of himself as well as how he compares himself to others.

"According to the "flow" experience theory; we are most absorbed, interested, and entertained when we are doing something that precisely matches our capabilities. When this happens, we experience a psychological state of flow, a total engagement with what we are doing."
-(Wegner, 1989, 70)

"I think about baseball when I wake up in the morning. I think about it all day and I dream about it at night. The only time I don't think about it is when I'm playing it."

-Carl Yastrzemski

6

Wins and Losses

Most—if not all—sports encompass wins and losses. How we respond to wins and losses says a lot about our character. Young baseball players must be taught to deal with wins and losses on an emotionally aware level. Not only will they experience the exhilarating feelings of an awe-inspiring victory but they will also feel the heartbreak of a painful loss. Aside from fellow teammates and coaches, parental guidance is of most importance during these times.

Wins and losses are handled differently depending on the age of the player. Wins and losses should not hold *too* much importance, especially with younger players. Over the years, I've heard parents babble in disgust about the recent performance of their son's team. They are usually dismayed by the win-loss record of the team and sometimes use it as a measuring stick to indicate the level of success of a season.

Would you like your son's team to win every game? Why,

of course. We all would! However, at the younger age groups the future of a baseball player's career is not dependent on his little league team's win-loss record. Could you imagine your son being a junior or senior at the high school level and being recruited by a college coach who inquired about his 12-year-old travel ball team's success?

Naturally, it's easier to handle wins with positivity, grace, and good sportsmanship. Our character is tested when things don't exactly go our way and we lose a hard-fought game or a "blowout." I acknowledge the competitive nature within us all, but to sulk over it will not help.

It's the parent that sets the tone when it comes to whether or not the child responds in a continuously negative way. The pain of a loss should only be temporary and short-lived.

Personal player development must always be top priority in the minds of parents in the baseball community. The refining and acquiring of individual skills is of utmost importance, along with making sure that the proper knowledge is gained that will help his performance at the next level.

> But Michael, are you saying that being a team player isn't all that important? Isn't it selfish to have my child's development at the forefront of what's considered most important?

What is a team player?

Oftentimes, many confuse being a "team player" with neglecting personal development. It is a myth that you must focus solely on the team rather than the individual. The fact of the matter is you can be the best team player you can be *while* putting a major focus on yourself as a baseball player.

In fact, being the very best you can be as a player is the most effective way to help your team. Parents often receive major backlash from other parents or coaches who don't understand the dynamic from this particular point of view.

This shouldn't be much of a worry, considering that most youth teammates don't end up playing on the same team later on down the line in their baseball careers (Middle School, Junior High or High School level). Teaching your son about the aspects of being a team player has its benefits, but it must be understood from a perspective that does not encourage him to neglect his personal development as a player.

"One of the beautiful things about baseball is that every once in a while you come into a situation where you want to, and where you have to, reach down and prove something."

-Nolan Ryan

7

Sportsmanship

A baseball player learns a universal life lesson through sportsmanship on the field: respect. Sportsmanship doesn't have to be looked at as *liking* your opponent, but it should be seen as having the *respect* for others as you compete to win. Oftentimes, parents have the need to enforce sportsmanship rules, but they usually fail to exemplify the model behavior that they expect from the players.

The best way for children to learn sportsmanship is through the parent. When parents act with dignity and respect towards other team parents, umpires, coaches, and players, the player then begins to gradually understand how to conduct himself.

While displaying good sportsmanship for your child, be sure to remember that the simple actions count. All it takes is a small gesture, like shaking hands after games or congratulating players on the other team when they make a spectacular play.

Children will often notice their parents yelling at umpires for perceived "bad calls" or talking down about coaches within earshot of the child. These types of actions can encourage bad sportsmanship.

A player will probably experience bad calls, feel jealous of other players, lose a hard-fought game in the last inning, and play for a coach that manages his team differently. However, reacting negatively to any of these situations will only produce more and more negativity. How the parent reacts serves as the blueprint for the child on how to handle these situations.

Here are some examples of a parent's negative reactions that can encourage bad sportsmanship:

- *Making negative remarks about the talent level of another teammate.*
- *Insinuating that the team coach is at fault for losing a game or streak of games.*
- *Yelling negative comments at a player during a game (even your own child).*
- *Engaging in arguments with parents on the other team.*

Some of these key points may seem obvious, but they happen far too often. Some of them are more subtle and could take some true self-awareness to avoid.

Now that we have taken a look at a few examples of infractions that would be bad examples of good sportsmanship, it is important to note the actions all parents should incorporate into their new patterns of thinking:

- *Speak positively about the performance of other players on the team.*

- *Encourage children to cheer for other teammates.*
- *Congratulate opponents when they make good plays.*
- *Display courteous behavior towards the parents from the other team.*
- *Emphasize that baseball is a game that is designed for kids to have fun.*

Always remind your child that others will not always follow the appropriate sportsmanship code and that this is not something that has to have an effect on them. How parents *react* to poor sportsmanship is just as important as how they *show* good sportsmanship. When parents notice someone exemplifying unnecessary taunting, foul play or any other examples of bad sportsmanship, it is important to mention it. This is the perfect time to explain why that certain behavior is uncalled for and why it will not be tolerated. Furthermore, parents should acknowledge when their children display the same sportsmanship that they encourage.

"Baseball is almost the only orderly thing in a very unorderly world. If you get three strikes, even the best lawyer in the world can't get you off."

-Bill Veeck

8

Contagious Attitudes

In baseball, infectious mindsets can be just as contagious as the common cold. Younger-aged ball players are susceptible to picking up both positive and negative attitudes from other teammates.

This is evident if you have ever witnessed a team's momentum shift take place. One game, the team's momentum is at an all-time high, fueled by a sense of passion and fun where everyone seems to be playing their best. The next, it may feel like a dark cloud descended over the dugout. This dynamic happens at all levels of baseball, from tee-ball to the Major Leagues. At any level, it is a challenge for a ball player to keep one mindset despite the changing energies of the team.

Of course, when things are going well for the team and things seem to be working on all cylinders, it is natural to ride that wave of momentum. Though this can be a good thing, it is when the transmittable mindset or attitude is one that can be harmful towards a player's performance that action needs to take place. Remaining a team player but breaking away from the "group mentality" that can plague a whole team is a challenge that is usually never discussed by those involved with the success of a ball player (coaches, parents, etc.).

This is vital to the mental aspect of a baseball player's game for the simple fact that baseball is a game that requires players to play against themselves. This may sound odd from a more practical perspective because a real-world pattern of thinking will say, *"Of course he's not playing against himself, silly. There are guys on the other team who he's competing against!"* But when a player understands that the best he can do is all he can do, pressure is alleviated and performance will accelerate.

It is best for the parent to be the "ground wire." Reiteration of expectations of on- and off-field attitude will instill a level of discipline that will develop a solid and unbreakable foundation. In other words, this will guarantee a stronger psychological defense that is much needed in baseball. As a parent, one of the most important bits of information you would have to offer would be to ensure the player knows not all teammates (and not all parents) will exemplify a prototypical attitude.

In a lengthy baseball career, it is likely that you will be placed on a team with individuals who have varying attitudes. These could be caused by many reasons, some of which include lack of confidence, imbalanced emotional states, jealousy, and being spoiled by their parents.

It would be helpful to use actual incidences that happen with other teammates as examples in order to differentiate between the right and wrong ways that players should handle themselves.

For example, if a teammate displays his frustration for

58

making a mistake by throwing a temper tantrum, talk about how the behavior was unacceptable and how it did not help solve the problem. It's most definitely better to use real examples of the non-exemplary behavior of others as a tool to teach your own player how to handle himself in future situations. Of course, do this in a respectful way that does not demean his teammates.

"The thing I like about baseball is that it's one-on-one. You stand up there alone, and if you make a mistake, it's your mistake. If you hit a home run, it's your home run."

-Hank Aaron

9

Why it is Important to Learn from the Best

I grew up without role models or older siblings who were able to teach me baseball on a more in-depth level. Since I was raised in Montgomery, Alabama, a city without a major professional sports team, I was left with no option but to root for the closest "home team" we had, the Atlanta Braves. Watching the Atlanta Braves games played a big role in learning the ins and outs of baseball.

Out of boredom and for sheer fun, I would imitate my favorite players. I picked up the way they ran, their batting stances, and how they threw the ball. Although I saw this as just something fun to do, I didn't initially realize that I was actually learning through my imitations.

The imagination I used to have fun and pass time would lead me to inadvertently pick up on valuable techniques and tools that would be advantageous in the long run. As time went on, I would learn important game strategies as I watched the games.

Listening to the in-game commentators as they revealed tidbits, game secrets, and various baseball lingo would familiarize me with lots of new, important concepts. I know I would not have learned as much as I did about the game if I had not watched Major League Baseball on television.

Watching professional players in action is the best non-physical way to stimulate growth in the development of a baseball player. Since the early 1990s, studies have been conducted by neurologists at the University of California, Los Angeles; the University of Parma in Italy; the University of Rome; and many other institutes to determine how the brain's motor neurons responds to seeing the actions of others. Numerous experiments have concluded that the same neurons in the brain that trigger during the completion of a physical action are the same neurons that are triggered when *watching* the same physical action take place (Schreiber, 2011). These studies are a great representation of how connected we are to the activities we watch, especially as spectators of sporting events. This is why some neurologists argue that the brain is unable to differentiate between *doing* and *watching*. Watching the game causes us to put ourselves in the game. This inspires us to use our minds to imagine ourselves on the field doing those things we see professional players do.

Think about when you learned to do your favorite dance. Unless you were the originator of this dance move, you saw someone else do it first. You carefully watched whoever it was doing the dance to study the body patterns and movements. This allowed your mind to process the information that your brain would then instruct your body to do. Even if you unknowingly did this, this is the process that took place.

After watching the body movements of others while doing a dance, you then attempted to imitate what you saw. You may not have been able to do it correctly right away, but with the combination of observing visually *and* practicing, it equated to eventually learning how to do it.

> But, Michael, I'm a huge baseball fan. I've been a Chicago Cubs fan since the age of eight. I barely miss a game every year, but I stunk as a baseball player and only made it through pee-wee ball. How do you explain this? If what you say about watching the game makes you better is true, why wasn't I able to become a great player?

How an individual watches is imperative. Watching for pure entertainment is fine; however, this is usually strictly for enjoyment and leisure purposes. Watching games from a more engaged and studious point of view with the intent to *learn* and *gain knowledge* is beneficial for a baseball player who is serious about reaching his full potential. Paying close attention to the in-game situations as they develop pitch by pitch stimulates the mind to learn and absorb.

After a decent amount of time is spent watching attentively, the pieces of the puzzle start to fit and more aspects of the game begin to make sense. Observing pitch count (number of balls and strikes), number of outs, number of runners that are currently on base, score, batting order, and other facets of the game are all keys in raising baseball acumen (or Baseball IQ).

Baseball I.Q. – unlike the most commonly known intelligence quotient (I.Q.), Baseball I.Q. does not consist of a numerical value. Baseball I.Q. is an intangible asset to a player that reflects his knowledge, ability to spot in-game situations, and his adaptability. Unlike natural talent level, Baseball I.Q. is a component that doesn't have a ceiling. It can be expanded as far as a player is willing to learn.

"Baseball is 90 percent mental—the other half is physical."
-Yogi Berra

There are many instances where young players (even players of older ages) learn from their peers. If their peers are playing the game the correct way, this is not a problem. However, more often than not, their peers are not going to have the proper technique, mindset, and work ethic to be effective in the long run. It is human nature to imitate those around us, and this is no exception.

I've often encountered many young ball players who watch little to no Major League Baseball on television. If you know a player has not received proper instruction from a reliable source and he does not watch the best players play, it is a no-brainer that he could only learn from his fellow teammates. It is impossible for a player to improve if he only observes incorrect practices of the game.

Bad swings, improper throwing motion, bad base running, and many other mistakes are all the result of this dynamic. As a parent, it is important to suggest sitting down as a family to watch a Major League game. Going to a game in person— whether it be Major League, college, or semi-professional—is an even better way to observe players at a higher level.

Whenever I speak to one of my younger trainees, I will usually ask them if they have watched any Major League baseball that particular week. If they have, I immediately ask, "What did you learn?" After expecting these types of questions from me upon arrival to our training sessions, they get in the habit of watching games as a student as opposed to watching as a spectator.

"Why does everyone stand up and sing Take Me Out to the Ball Game when they're already there?"

-Larry Anderson

10

Being a Versatile Player

A t some point in a career, baseball players will play multiple positions for their team. Whether the team needs him to play many positions or he wants to stay well-rounded as a ball player, this is something that will have to be dealt with sooner or later. Having the flexibility to play a number of positions is one of the great, underrated assets a player brings to the table.

As a private instructor, I get questions from inquisitive parents all the time about whether their child should stick with one position versus another (or both). Here are some reasons why the need to play multiple positions will come about in the first place:

1. Your child is second best on the team in his primary position

Example: Your son has played shortstop as a primary position every year of his little league career. You have just tried out for a new team, and the current shortstop happens to be better (which most parents are often too afraid to admit), forcing your son to play at his secondary position.

2. You play for a coach who moves players out of position frequently

It is very likely (especially with younger age groups) that your child will *need* to know more than one position on the field due to his teammates getting moved around after every change in pitcher. This depends on how many reliable pitchers are on the team.

3. Absent Teammates

Whether it is due to vacation, sickness, or quitting the team, there are many reasons why a teammate will have to miss a game or two. This will automatically change the lineup around and force the coach to make some defensive and offensive changes. This may cause your child to play in a strange or uncomfortable position.

Being that *all* of the instances above can happen over the course of a season, it is crucial that your son be well versed in multiple positions.

Even if your son excels behind the plate as a catcher, there may be a tournament that requires three back-to-back-to-back games in the middle of the summer. In this situation, heat exhaustion is a definite concern, and, therefore, safety should be put before position preference and another catcher should enter the game. This is a prime example of why younger players have no way around playing multiple positions.

As a player gets older, he possesses more added value in the eyes of coaches, scouts, and recruiters if he can play many positions well. At high school, college, and professional-level baseball, these types of players who can play multiple positions are deemed *utility players*. Utility players (in older age groups) usually tend to catch the eye of a recruiter more frequently since they can potentially fill in at multiple spots on the field. A player can be considered a "utility outfielder" who plays all outfield positions (right, center and left). The same holds true for a "utility infielder," a player who is proficient at most—or all—of the infield positions. Even though they are rare, there are players who are both utility infield and outfield players.

For a younger player, being seen by a recruiter may not be an immediate concern, but even players who are looking to make an elite travel or all-star team in their local area should be utility players. Being able to play more than one position on the field will increase a player's chances of making it into the starting line-up.

Baseball, like many other sports, is a game of adjustments. Too often, athletes get forced out of baseball due to an inability to adjust to new team circumstances.

Let's see how playing multiple positions is an advantage:

Todd has been playing baseball since the age of six. All throughout his little league career, he has played at first base. Since Todd has great hands and above average hand-eye coordination, his coaches have always chosen to play him primarily at first base. Everyone raves about how great Todd's catching skills are at the position, and his parents are happy about the recognition he receives for his skills. By the time Todd is 13, his peers are all reaching puberty at a faster rate than he is. Since first base is usually a position held by bigger and stronger players, Todd's new travel ball coach for his 13-year-old team is hesitant to let him prove himself at first base. With no prior experience at any other positions, Todd is left as a back-up option and forced to watch the game from the bench for majority of the season.

This is a perfect example of why parents should think ahead to potential situations like this. If players are not well rounded and well versed in different areas, they can potentially be handicapped.

Thankfully, some positions are "interchangeable" in the respect that they are very similar in style and what's required.

For example, shortstop and second base are two positions that are very similar. The only difference is the required length of the throw that each position has to make over to first base. All outfield positions will have to catch fly balls and ground balls in nearly the same capacity. The main difference between the three is that center field has to be able to cover more space in the outfield.

Catcher is a position that is not as easily interchangeable as the rest of the positions on the field. This would be considered a "fixed position," requiring specific skills.

If your team coach is adamant about putting a player (especially at a very young age) in only one position, this doesn't mean that you cannot work on other positions outside of regularly scheduled practices and games to prepare for future possibilities. Find time to keep the skills in other positions intact. If you have a trainer, let them know that you would like to do some work on both the primary and secondary position (maybe third or fourth position as well).

Knowing multiple positions is also a great way to enhance Baseball I.Q. Being well versed in various positions will get a player in tune with where everyone is supposed to be on each play throughout the game. This will help team chemistry and will help things run a lot smoother.

Switch hitting

Being a switch hitter, a player with the ability to swing right-handed and left-handed, shows great versatility as a player. Switch-hitting baseball players are a valued commodity for any team. Switch hitters have the advantage when it comes to pitcher-hitter match-ups. This allows them to not be at a disadvantage when it comes to breaking pitches like curveballs or sliders (normally this applies to older age groups who have the ability to throw these types of pitches).

The younger the player, the more parents should lean towards the option of learning to switch hit. Since children learn quickly at early ages, this is the perfect time to introduce hitting on both sides of the plate. It is best to avoid setting a deadline on players becoming proficient on both sides. If the player is determined to be an effective switch hitter, they can succeed with hard work and dedication. I've often seen players give up on the hopes of ever "getting it," but it may take a fairly long time for hitting on both sides to feel natural.

Being versatile and adaptable are the main ingredients to surviving in baseball. If your player is against learning to be multidimensional, thoroughly explain to them these aforementioned benefits to help them understand its importance.

"Baseball players are smarter than football players. How often do you see a baseball team penalized for too many men on the field?"

-Jim Bouton

11

How to
Handle Slumps

"Tough times never last; tough people always do."
– Robert Schuller

The term "slump" usually refers to a "hitting slump." We usually correlate batting performance with someone's "batting average," a way to keep up with a player's success numerically. Slumps are not only in reference to batting average; they could also translate into pitching or fielding slumps (making errors and bad judgments consecutively).

Slumps are merely impossible to avoid and are an inescapable part of baseball, and a misunderstanding of this truth could cause frustration and confusion. Often parents get emotionally caught up in the attachment of a child's individual success. Though this is understandable because of the love and admiration within the parent-child relationship, it is important to formulate a strategic plan to avoid a long-term slump.

Note: Emphasis must always be put on <u>shortening</u> a slump rather than preventing it.

Since children strive for acceptance, it is imperative that a parent react to slumps in a mature and constructive manner. Reacting immaturely to a prolonged slump will only add more unneeded pressure to the player. During this time, not only are players frustrated that they are not playing their best but they are also embarrassed by striking out, walking batters, or missing ground balls and fly balls consecutively. It is possible for you to be a helping hand in this situation. By thinking on a higher level, you could exploit this misfortune as an opportunity to teach valuable life lessons.

Sometimes slumps can be "misdiagnosed." We may all think that it is obvious what a slump is, but someone without a moderate, fundamental understanding of the game may consider getting a hit three out of 10 times to be a poor ratio. When it comes to other sports, being successful three out of 10 times looks like a terrible performance. *Example: A quarterback in football completing 3 of 10 passes or a basketball player making 3 of 10 free throws.* As it pertains to baseball, getting a hit 30% (or hitting for an average of .300) of the time during a Major League career will more than likely get you into the Hall of Fame. If you were not previously aware, hopefully that example should give you a better understanding of how difficult it is to excel at the game.

What is Failure?

Can you always diagnose a slump based on batting average? Sometimes you can, but definitely not always. For example, when a player hits a hard line drive right at a defender and gets out, is that a failed at-bat? If a player happens to hit three hard line-drives right at defenders in *one* game and goes zero for three (zero hits in three official at-bats), did he have a bad game? **The end result of an at-bat or a game (statistically speaking) is not always indicative of a good or bad performance.**

This is extremely important to understand because parents must remind players about this dynamic. Since baseball is a team sport, successful at-bats may not always result in a base hit. A ground out to move the runner ahead, a pop-fly to score a run from third base, or a sacrifice bunt to advance another player are all great team at-bats. They do not make batting averages improve, but reminding young players how important great team at-bats are lessen discouragement about getting out while helping the team.

In baseball, there is such a thing as a "good out" that can help the team win. It's imperative to forget about the numbers and focus on having good plate appearances. Understanding this will also help *you* as a parent with not getting agitated because you think your child is "failing" when they are actually having productive at-bats. This is why having at least a minimal level of knowledge of the game is so imperative.

Solutions

Don't create information overload!

When a player gets into a slump, everyone seems to have a solution for the problem, such as:

- "Your bat is too heavy. Choke up!"
- "Your elbow needs to be bent *this* way."

- "Turn your feet *this* way."

These are not the only solutions. Though some slumps derive from problems in physical technique, a lot of slumps are the offspring of a flawed mental approach. Don't obsess or be nit-picky about what should be done to fix a slump. Whether the solution is a mental or mechanical one, make sure the *simplest* solution is used initially. Don't overload a player with *too* much data to process. This will cause him to over think his mechanics and could result in regression.

Get help from a private instructor

Since advice from too many sources at once can prove to be overwhelming for a player trying to get back on track, it is a good idea to find a trusted private baseball instructor to help the player get out of a slump. The chosen instructor should be able to give you informative feedback that is specific to your child (More details on private instruction later). It's also no secret that children tend to listen more to non-parental advisories in certain areas.

A private trainer provides an influx of new information that can begin the process of refocusing the mind through solid, physical action steps. It may or may not create drastic changes in the beginning, but regardless of the immediate outcome, it will create momentum in the direction a player desires.

It is most important to make sure that the slump does not fester or worsen for too long in order to preserve confidence and self-esteem. As performance slips and pressure to excel starts to creep in, the chances of internalizing failure are much higher.

Dangers of Internalizing Failure

There are many ways in which a baseball player begins to internalize failure. A coach's opinion, words from a parent, recent on-field performances, and a lack of playing time are only a few examples. Once a player starts to internalize failure, it starts to become an expectation for *himself*. At this point, to fail becomes somewhat normal. This is when a player can begin to sabotage his own opportunities for success. This causes a player to not seek opportunities to learn from mistakes or play to the best of his ability. The main challenge in reversing this is to get a player to disassociate himself with who he *thinks* he is as a ball player, which is often a false depiction of his true talent level.

The ups and downs and peaks and valleys of a baseball season can make a player feel like a Hall-of-Famer one minute and the world's worst player the next. With a positive and powerful inner knowledge of his true potential, he is then equipped to fend off any feelings of disempowerment or discouragement.

This is the difference between a player thinking to himself "I am a bad player" or "I am a good player who is experiencing some rough times right now."

The parent's attitude is a vital factor in how a player sees himself. This is especially true for younger players. Engaging in constructive conversation is essential in finding out how they are thinking. This will help gauge where they are in their positive or negative internalization. Rarely is any attention needed for a player who has internalized a positive message within himself, even if that message may be overly confident (beyond his current abilities).

A parent can normally tell when their child is internalizing failure, not performing at their highest level, or lacking self-esteem. Parents must take the time to monitor and improve a player's mental-emotional state.

When a player thoroughly analyzes how he feels about a bad situation, the problem tends to lose its magnitude. Getting to the root of the emotion they feel when they are in a slump of any kind is the first step to getting back on the right path. From my personal interaction with hundreds of parents, I've seen that most do not take the time to find out how the player is feeling during these rough patches. They are usually too busy being consumed by their own frustrations over what they would consider an unsatisfactory performance. This is one of the many reasons why this game is not just a challenge for the player but also for the parent. This is another reason why being very conscientious of your actions and reactions is key.

Slumps are like Boa Constrictors: the more you struggle, the tighter it gets.

When things are not going the way a player would like—on the mound or at the plate—trying *harder* seems like you are attempting to sprint full speed in quick sand. Adding unnecessary pressure can prolong slumps rather than end them.

Getting your son focused on the *now* can help improve slumps. Parents must send the message that the past must be left behind. The past should only be discussed when it serves a meaningful purpose that is absolutely relevant to the present. Therefore, we cannot harp on past failures—even if they occurred yesterday.

> *So are you telling me that I shouldn't talk to my son about yesterday's game? I thought it would be a good idea since I could use it as an opportunity to reflect on mistakes that might help him get better.*

Speaking of a past performance, as said before, must be done under the guise of extracting lessons that can assist players in the present and future. When speaking of the past, you must be careful to avoid passing judgment. At times, a lecture from a parent to a player about his past woes can help strengthen the internalized failure previously mentioned. That is why *skillful reflection* is of utmost importance.

Skillful reflection should include questions like:

- "What do you think you could have done better on that play?"
- "If you are in a similar situation next game, what should be your reaction?"
- "What do you think the reason was for not executing properly during your second at-bat?"
- "It seems that you were struggling to find your strike zone on the mound. Do you feel like that might have had something to do with the way you warmed up before the game?"
- "Listen, I know things aren't going too well for you out on the field as of late. Is there anything I can do to help?"

Saying nothing at all about a current slump could be just as detrimental as saying too much. Normally, a young player will use their imagination to conclude how a parent is thinking about their performance, which is why not saying anything at all during a slump is not advised either. Asking reflective questions gives you the power of letting the player know that you care and that you are focused on their success without potentially giving out false information that may work against what they are trying to accomplish.

When going through a slump, remembering a time when you were playing much better will help to imagine more successful performances. The thoughts of more successful performances will then begin to match the desire for improvement. This is where the beginning of improvement takes place. Sometimes the desire is already there, and all that is needs to be realized is the *belief* that it's possible.

*"Baseball is like a poker game.
Nobody wants to quit when
he's losing; nobody wants you
to quit when you're ahead."*

-Jackie Robinson

12

The Importance
of Extra Practice

"Practice makes ~~perfect~~ confidence"

Haven't we all heard this cliché phrase for as long as we can remember? Although it's very true when referring to physical skills, the effects of extra work on the game is downplayed from a psychological stand point (more later).

"The more I practice, the luckier I get." - Gary Player

Repetition, Repetition, Repetition!

Repetition is both the mother of all learning and a source of ultimate confidence. This is extremely important in baseball, a sport that is contingent upon confidence.

Nervousness and uncertainty usually come from a lack of preparation. Being nervous about a test or not looking forward to giving a presentation to an audience are prime examples of situations where repetition could help. A lack of repetition in baseball can cause a sense of anxiety that will negatively affect one's performance.

Baseball players in the developmental stages of learning are like children who are learning to ride a bike. Chances are after they have gotten over the initial scrapes and bruises from falling off the bike, they are confident about their abilities to ride a bike due to the practiced repetition. Repetition allows them to make mistakes as a means of "getting it out of their system."

Remember: mistakes are always better to be made in private, i.e. team practice, at-home, and private sessions rather than in the game.

How does confidence develop from repetition?

Extra time spent practicing will translate into more and more confidence. Imagine if a player spent an extra twenty minutes a day for five days a week working on a particular skillset. This adds up to an hour and forty minutes of *extra* practice in just one week. In one month, a child could do up to an extra seven hours of practice outside of their regularly scheduled training. Whether on a conscious or subconscious level, stepping onto the field knowing you have out-worked majority of players you are competing against will *automatically* give you a psychological edge.

"We are what we repeatedly do.
Excellence then, is not an act, but a habit." -Aristotle

Visualization

Visualization is a practice that is one of the least talked-about tools that players can use to develop skills. Visualization is one of the best non-physical ways to enhance performance. As great philosophers and teachers from ancient to present day say, everything in physical form was once visualized in the mind.

Knowing this, we can encourage young ball players to *imagine* being successful on the field. Most people daydream about being successful at many things, but to consciously envision one's self accomplishing feats and other desired actions on the field will work wonders in what's called **mental rehearsal**.

Mental rehearsal works exactly the way it sounds; it is mentally rehearsing all that can or will take place physically. This form of extra practice is not identified as *real* practice, but can be an effective tool to supplement physical practice. This process works similarly to how watching games, as mentioned previously in the "Why it is Important to Learn from the Best" chapter, can stimulate the nervous system through vivid imagination.

In other sports, you can see players going through mental rehearsal *during* their performances. For example, world famous golfer Tiger Woods often kneels down behind the golf ball to get a picture of how he must hit the ball. With his intensely focused stare, you can *see* that he is calculating how he will approach his next shot. His mental rehearsal includes envisioning himself hitting the ball with a certain level of force to send it in a particular direction.

Gymnasts also stare intently at the balance beam before hopping on. In these moments, they practice their routines and techniques in their minds before they even start their performance.

Baseball is a game of mistakes; therefore, practice does not make perfect in this case. However, it will enhance self-confidence and performance while decreasing anxiety, doubt, and uncertainty during game-time. So we can assume that "**Practice makes confidence**."

While extra practice is important, it is even more crucial that practice sessions focus on quality rather than quantity. *Proper practice* should be the priority. A lack of quality repetition will rob a player of reaching his full potential.

"Hard work beats talent when talent doesn't work hard."

-Tim Notke

13

Quality
Practice Habits

Practice is imperative to success on the playing field; however, the importance of exercising the *proper* practice methods tends to slip the minds of most parents. Now, this mishap is not purposely committed. This dynamic is just something that is rarely brought to the attention of most baseball parents. The majority of parents, when taking a child to practice, assume that the time spent practicing is used productively. Making this assumption can prove to be detrimental if we do not make sure that the player is doing the practice repetitions *correctly*.

Here is an example of a situation that could occur:

> Jimmy has struggled at the plate lately. In order to prevent him from going into a deeper slump, his mom and dad decide to take him to the batting cages to see some balls and take a few swings. They arrive to their local batting cage and rent a thirty-minute time slot with a machine. With no prior examination of his swing or on-site expert supervision, Jimmy takes a few rounds off of the machine. He's sweaty and exhausted from the energy he's exerted over the

30-minute session. The parents and Jimmy both feel a sense of accomplishment upon going home, feeling that they have taken the necessary steps in bettering Jimmy's performance.

Being around baseball for years, I understand that this story resonates with many people. Either you have taken these steps to achieve improvement, or you know of other parents who have done something similar. Let's analyze a situation like this from a logical perspective.

Notice in the story I mentioned "with no prior examination of his swing or on-site expert supervision." This indicates that we are unaware if Jimmy is even swinging *correctly*. Let's say it is his technique that is suffering and causing the problem with his performance. How will we know without a proper diagnosis or evaluation of his current swing pattern? Not knowing this and still allowing Jimmy to step into the batting cage and *repeat* what could possibly be an out-of-whack swing could do major harm to his technique.

Using the machine pitch batting cage could be either a good or bad thing, depending on if it is used properly. I personally do not recommend using fast pitch machines for hitting practice *until* the mechanics of the swing have a solid fundamental foundation. The reason why is because when a child steps into what feels like a "live" or "game" situation, they become result-oriented and will do whatever it takes to obtain a satisfactory outcome. The emphasis of proper mechanics and form are then placed on the back burner. Making good contact with a few pitches without using the proper form in the cage can create a false sense of confidence and accomplishment that will not help the player in the long run. It is important to remember the machine isn't capable of communicating to you what's wrong with your swing if you are experiencing a problem with technique.

Quality vs. Quantity

Although I briefly presented a situation where a child had a batting technique problem, the concept of quality vs. quantity is universal and can pertain to pitching or fielding as well. The bottom line is that *quality* is most important when practicing. This means twenty quality swings, fielded ground balls, or pitches are *far* better than 100 repetitions of each done in poor form. As a parent, if you do not have the necessary knowledge of exactly how or what your child should do to achieve quality repetitions that build solid fundamental mechanics, it doesn't mean that you will not be able to find a trusted private instructor to help (more information in the next chapter).

Of course, taking your child to the batting cage unattended by an expert may be cheaper and more cost effective, but like in anything in life, "you get what you pay for." Cutting corners and trying to take the easy way out may prove to be detrimental to your child. Once your child builds a solid foundation of technique, you may be able to get expert training *periodically*.

Pitching is definitely a part of the game that needs to be done correctly, for two reasons: to perform well *and* to prevent injury. There could be a slight fault in a pitcher's motion that may cause his arm to maneuver in a way that could put pressure or stress on a particular joint or tendon (more information in the chapter on injury).

Fundamentals are the key ingredient to becoming a better player. Working on getting better without working on basic fundamentals would be equivalent to an architect who pays little attention to the foundation of the building but spends a lot of time working on a skyscraper.

"Baseball is the only field of endeavor where a man can succeed three times out of ten and be considered a good performer."

-Ted Williams

14

Private Instruction

Selecting the right private instructor for baseball could be similar to choosing the right hair stylist, fitness trainer, mechanic, or any other designated specialist. When you invest your money to get a desired result, you want someone who is trustworthy and knowledgeable in that field of service. This is no different when choosing an instructor for baseball. Most parents don't have the capability or the skill to help make their young ball players better in areas where they may lack ability, but there is nothing wrong with that.

Getting the much-needed help from elsewhere shows that the parent is serious about providing beneficial guidance for their child. A parent allowing their ego to convince them that they don't need a trainer or can do it themselves could prove to be detrimental if the parent is inexperienced on proper technique, philosophy, or strategy. Here are some valuable tips that will help you in your quest to finding the right baseball instructor for your child.

An Instructor Should Have a Credible Background

To assure that your time and money is well spent, make sure that the instructor you choose to train your child possesses extensive knowledge of the overall game of baseball. More specifically, it is essential that the instructor be well versed in the specialty upon which you would like your son to improve. For example, if you would like your child to get batting training, find someone who spent most of their career as a successful hitter.

Although many former pitchers know enough to teach young players about batting, it's always best to learn from someone who dedicated more time to a particular area of the game (this goes for former batters teaching young pitchers as well). You may have already found a trusted instructor to train your son in a particular area that he didn't have personal experience with. If you are getting the desired results, stick with them.

A credible background is necessary. The question is: how credible? Oftentimes, parents have the misconception that an instructor must have an overly qualified background to be a good coach. This sometimes means that they would prefer that an instructor with a former background in professional baseball (which could also mean minor league or semi-professional) train their child. This is a valid thought to have, since most of us naturally believe that playing at a high level would constitute having a thorough knowledge of the game.

Although many times this is true, one thing that we must realize is that not everyone who has played at a higher or "professional" level of the game has the capacity to *teach* the game effectively. Being proficient at conveying information and breaking down concepts while having the ability to work with young ball players is essential. This mainly deals with *personality*, which does not hinge on past personal performance on the playing field.

An Instructor Must Educate the Parent

Many parents do not have an idea as to what is needed to help their child improve when it comes to proper training. A *thorough* trainer will observe the player and then point out what skills need improvement during an evaluation in the early stages of training. If no evaluation has occurred, make sure you ask the right questions. As a parent who spends their hard-earned money to get results out of this investment, you have every right to ask questions.

The Right Questions to Ask

You don't have to be a baseball connoisseur to have a constructive conversation about your child's progression. A good trainer will not try to stomp you with crazy, over-the-top lingo and baseball logic to confuse you. A trainer who is fairly knowledgeable should be able to explain baseball philosophy, training technique, and strategy in a simple fashion that is easy to understand. After all, they will be teaching your child the game, so it is important that they are able to convey the information in a way that will allow *anyone* to understand it. Here are some general questions that may help you get the right answers you need from your trainer:

- "Is my child listening attentively during lessons?"
- "What is the most important thing that my child needs to work on to get better?"
- "Is there anything we can do at home to speed up the learning process in between scheduled sessions?"
- "How often should we come for training in order to see the greatest amount of improvement?"

If you have questions about equipment (gloves, bats, etc.) use the instructor as a resource for feedback. For example, if you have multiple bats that your child uses interchangeably and you aren't exactly sure which one to stick with consistently, ask the trainer to observe the player's swing while using different bats. This also applies for different gloves and other equipment.

Be sure that you are respectful of the instructor's time. Sometimes they have a few extra minutes before or after a session to answer questions. If you notice that the instructor has a session scheduled with another client immediately after the session with your child, be courteous and get back with them at a more convenient time. It may be better to call or make an appointment with the instructor during their off hours to address any concerns that require a more lengthy conversation. Emailing may also be a useful tool.

Pricing/ Rates

Sometimes it is difficult to find an affordable instructor. Of course, whether you can afford the instructor's rate is going to be up to your discretion. Keep in mind that private training fees vary based on a trainer's experience and reputation, facility prices and geographic location and area.

Regardless of fees, the investment will certainly be well worth the price if you find an instructor who can provide results. Like the saying goes, "pay now or pay later." If you are on a more personal level with your instructor you may be able to get discounted for lessons by recommending new clients. Most instructors reward current clients who help drive new business.

Respect the Journey

Do not bring your child to a trainer in a short period of time prior to tryouts and expect a miracle. I've personally seen this happen too many times. Training takes time. The process must be respected or the price will most certainly be paid in full. Considering that baseball is a more "skill-required" sport that is contingent upon refinement of expertise, it will take a steady diet of concentration and focus spanning over a longer period of time to yield desired results. I recall a parent walking into my training facility one day telling me that his son needed a "quick tune-up" right before an important tryout he was on the way to. What example would you be setting for your child with this type of behavior? When things like this happen and the player is struggling or not able to play at a high level, the parent should be able to to share the blame.

Easy on the Put-downs

Lots of parents unconsciously spew words of disempowerment in reference to their child in conversation with others, oftentimes while the child is in the vicinity. From a psychological perspective, listening to your parent give a demoralizing review of your recent undesirable performance is a blow to the spirit. Countless times I've heard parents gripe in front of their sons.

"Well, Todd is just not doing anything right these past three games. He's popping everything up, left and right. When he does make contact it's not solid at all and he can't seem to catch up to speed with the fastballs. I'm bringing him to you because he just won't listen to me anymore and I'm tired of telling him!"

If you feel the need to give the instructor a heads up on some specific problems, take them aside and speak with them discretely. A player hearing their frustrated parent rant about how poorly they have been performing is extremely discouraging and may cause serious damage to a player's performance.

Benefits of Private Training

Aside from skill improvement, there are a host of other notable benefits that come with seeing a personal baseball instructor.

1. **Player-specific attention** - Oftentimes a player will not get the coaching necessary to address more unique problems or habits when practicing in a team setting. This often doesn't happen intentionally and a coach is not at fault for this. This usually happens by mere design.

    While conducting a team practice, it is challenging to give the needed, specified attention to all players within the allotted practice time, especially if the time constraints are limited. Private instruction offers an opportunity to have personal needs of the player addressed. All players are not created equal; therefore, they all need their own special attention that caters to their style of hitting, throwing, fielding, and technique.

2. **Self-recognition** - Due to the aforementioned time constraints, it is important for a player to understand and recognize his own faults when they happen. After a series of good private sessions, a player will begin to have a better self-awareness and understanding of when they are doing things correctly versus when they are doing them incorrectly. Being able to correct your own mistakes and to become your own coach is the key to becoming a more mature baseball player.

3. **Mental Blueprint** - Private instruction provides a mental blueprint on *how* things are supposed to be done. Most coaches and parents put total emphasis on *what* it is a player is supposed to do, and they neglect to question if what is being done is being done properly. A private instructor will give a player a mental guideline from which he needs to work so that he is equipped to practice correctly when expert supervision is not around.

How to get the Most out of Your Private Lessons

1. **Value Your Time and Money** - To ensure you get your money's worth, you must do your part in making sure that as much time as possible is used towards a productive session. This, of course, starts with being on time for the lesson, which is important. However, being *early* would be a lot more beneficial.

This will allow time for warm-up, stretching, and other preparation so that from the beginning, the time used will be used productively. Doing things like helping pick up baseballs in between drills can also a very useful way to get as much practice time in as possible.

I once heard a dad tell a player, "Son, I don't pay to watch you pick up baseballs!" as he helped him to gather baseballs in the batting cage. I agree with his statement and I feel like every parent should feel the same way in regards to getting more 'bang for your buck.' However, this is just a suggestion and could be based solely off of personal preference. I have known parents who opted to simply keep a distance from the instructor and the player during training sessions. That is fine as well.

2. **Homework -** No, we're not talking about schoolwork. We are talking about baseball homework, which is what all serious baseball players who wish to improve should do. Going back to what I mentioned earlier in "Ask the Right Questions," ask what specific drills your son can work on at home that may not require a lot of professional supervision or equipment.

This will help speed up the process of progression and also shorten the learning curve. Doing "baseball homework" in between scheduled training sessions will keep concepts learned from the lesson fresh on the player's mind. Only practicing during lessons or team practice would be the equivalent of going to school every day without studying and doing extra assignments at home.

3. **Keep it consistent** - A long layoff could lead to skill atrophy, which may deplete what was previously learned. Finding a reasonable schedule that keeps lessons consistent will be best for optimal development. A player who trains sparingly and at random increments will not always reach his full potential.

4. **Session Timeframe** - I highly recommend that longer time slots be used in the first few initial lessons with a new instructor as a means of getting the player acclimated to the instructor's use of terminology, drills, pace, and teaching style. This will allow an instructor to slow things down and explain vital and new concepts in a more easy-to-learn fashion.

   This approach will also assist in the establishment of muscle memory. Once this is established and all parties feel that the player has reached a level of greater understanding in what he has learned, then the option of scheduling shorter time slots could be entertained. (Example: Most private trainers/facilities offer time slots for purchase in 30- or 60-minute increments.)

5. **Utilize "Learning through Teaching"** - *"The best test of whether or not you really understand a concept is trying to teach it to someone else. Teaching calls for complete understanding of the concept."* - Richard Rusczyk

   We all remember being assigned a particular subject to present to the class during our school days. After teaching the subject to the class, it was much easier to understand.

That is because this encourages you to see and learn things from a whole new perspective, which speeds up the process of learning (Rusczyk, 2013).

After each session, perhaps on the way home or upon arrival, ask the player thought-provoking questions about the lesson that just took place. This will get the brain focused on stimulating memory of what was taught. Get your child to show you what proper techniques were taught. Take it a step further by getting them to teach it to you. I can say that after becoming a private instructor myself, I've learned much more about how to play the game from teaching it than I ever did while playing.

Important Things to Keep in Mind

Developing a personal yet professional relationship with your child's private baseball instructor is very important. Trust your instincts. Ask yourself if you think your child could get along well with the trainer and whether you think the trainer is genuinely interested in helping your child improve. The private instructor you select should motivate your child through using positive, not negative, reinforcement. However, do not confuse *discipline* with negative reinforcement. It is essential that whatever instructor you select will hold your player accountable.

As a trainer, I personally would not feel that I am doing right by the parent if I did not have a sense of respect for the time, money, and energy invested. Making sure that a player gets the most out of every session could involve some good old-fashioned tough love, which usually tends to equate to push-ups for most of my clients.

There may be times where the information from the instructor conflicts or differs from that of the team coach. To put a stranglehold on confusion, it is wise to let the team coach know that your son receives lessons from a qualified source with whom you are happy. By no means should you come across as "Hey, I've been taking Billy to train with someone who actually knows what they are talking about!"

Speak with the team coach and come up with a reasonable solution if ideas conflict. However, you should never let a coach (especially one who may not have qualified expertise) bully you into not getting outside help. This is usually the type of coach who feels like his players should *only* get advice from *him*. After all, he may not even be your son's coach in the following season(s), if we are thinking long-term.

Lastly, it is important that you don't try to impress a trainer with everything you know or *think* you know about baseball. On the other hand, don't feel embarrassed about a lack of knowledge. If done the right way, it is a learning experience for everyone and should be treated as such.

*"It's supposed to be hard.
If it wasn't hard, everyone
would do it. The hard is
what makes it great."*

-A League of Their Own

15

Evolution: Handling Changes in Fundamental Technique

There is not one baseball player who has maintained the same swing from the beginning to the end of his career. If you play the game long enough, it's only natural that your swing evolve as you make adjustments and changes. Unless a player started tee ball with the perfect swing, which is probably impossible, he will go through what I call a *Swing Evolution*.

It is essential to have a full understanding of the fact that a player's technique or style will change, break down, and rebuild unpredictably. At least one parent a week, usually in a state of semi-panic, explains to me that their son has "all of a sudden" changed up his style of hitting or fielding and decided to add or subtract what was once a component of his playing style. I always remind them of the continual process of getting to know one's self as a player. Many times in a player's career, his initial style of play (from earliest ages) mirrors what he's been taught by a parent or coach.

Although basic core fundamentals should be the foundation of all players' techniques, we must keep in mind that all players will naturally go through a phase where they add their own personal element in an attempt to find their comfort zone. Experimentation may be an ongoing process for certain players. This especially happens in cases where a player may be going through an extensive slump and is looking to change things up in hopes for better luck. Don't be surprised if a noticeable change occurs even when the player is playing well.

Not all changes in fundamental technique are unprovoked. Depending on what coach or private instructor your son is working with, it might be suggested that he change his strategic approach or other techniques such as arm motion during pitch delivery, leg kick before swinging, or body positioning while fielding.

Baseball is a game that requires one to continuously strive toward perfection. Many Major League baseball players hit countless amounts of baseballs off of the hitting tee every day in pursuit of the perfect swing. Most would agree that they will never ever get to that "perfect swing." Finding the arm slot, stride, or mechanics that works best for the player is a process. Throughout the highest ranks of amateur or professional baseball, pitchers are always watching film and doing drills to perfect lessons in the game that they've been taught as children.

Getting rid of old habits

Learning new habits involves dealing with behavioral and neurological patterns. Since our neurological patterns vary and our muscle memory differs, it's impossible to know how long it will take to break old bad habits and build new ones. Of course, you would have to take into account just how long the player has been practicing the bad habits and how much training or proper instruction is being implemented to fix it. Bad habits can be hard to break away from due to the comfort that it brings. Being familiar with doing things a certain way, even if they do not bring desired results, makes bad habits hard to break away from. There are just as many—or more—obstacles to fixing mental habits than physical ones.

"You are negatively influenced by two major hindrances: One is the influence of others; the other is the influence of your own old habits...You have developed patterns of thinking, so you can easily fall into those old habitual patterns rather than think the new thought that is in harmony with the new desire." -Law of Attraction by Esther and Jerry Hicks

I have seen players learn a new concept and then revert back to old bad habits. If a player is going through the process of learning a new concept but still doesn't seem to grasp it after a while, it would be good to slow things down and concentrate on fundamental movements.

If a player learns a new concept in a private lesson or from a team coach, that new concept should always initially be practiced at a slow pace rather than full speed. Newly introduced ways of performing a technique is always best learned when broken down into slower steps. This would be the same as expecting a five-year-old to know how to tie his or her shoe at full speed after *just* learning how to do it the week prior.

A prime example would be when a personal trainer

works with a particular client who has an issue with his hitting mechanics. Maybe he has an issue with not turning his back foot while swinging, which is an important part of the swing that helps him use the power in his legs. If the trainer sees that he has trouble remembering what to do to fix the problem, the trainer should make it a point to let him know that he has "homework" to do before the next time he comes in to do a session. The student should get in front of the mirror and practice turning his back foot as he swings in *slow* motion. This will help with closing the gap between the mind and body and help them to function in a much more synchronized way. Here is an example of a good regimen that a personal trainer could give a private student, with the percentages representing at what speed the player should exert his effort during the drill:

- 15 repetitions at 25% (Slowest)
- 20 repetitions at 50% (Half speed)
- 25 repetitions at 75% (Moderate Speed)
- 30 repetitions at 100% (Full speed)

For example, "20 reps at 50%" would have the player doing twenty repetitions of a particular movement at half speed.

Being Patient

Parents often put a silent timeline on when exactly they should see improvement. You should understand that it is natural for baseball players to go through these stages of evolving and getting to know who they are as unique and individual players. There will be ups and downs in this process. If a player works hard and remains dedicated, he will be able to fight through any low times during the process.

Parents must always understand to relax and allow the process to take place. It takes much time, work, and patience. There are many gifted athletes who were never discovered because they had never taken the time to allow their development to take place. In baseball, it is impossible to reach perfection, but a player can strive to become as great as he can be.

When detoxifying bad habits, each player must go through the process of the five R's:

1. **Recognize** when a bad habit seems to be forming before it gets to a point of doing extensive damage.

2. **Remove** the habits by acknowledging what needs to be fixed and beginning the process of working towards a solution.

3. **Replace** the old, ineffective habits with a new plan of action.

4. **Reinvent** by tweaking and making adjustments to the new approach until a happy medium is reached that feels comfortable.

5. **Repeat** the new habits enough times through high quality practice to drown out old habits.

"The other sports are just sports. Baseball is a love."

-Bryant Gumbel

16

The Truth
About Bats

*"The player makes the bat.
The bat doesn't make the player."*

Parents have asked me many questions about bats over the years. Which brand is best? Which is more durable? Is alloy or composite better? Does it matter what type of grip the bat has?

At a young age, a baseball player's performance is not contingent upon what brand or type of bat they use. Proper batting technique should be the ultimate focus of a player when it comes to hitting. With the onslaught of advertisement and the pressure from friends on the team to be "cool," most young players beg and plead for a bat that is most popular at that point in time. An intriguing name and paint design on a bat will immediately convince a child that they *need* to buy it to enhance their performance. This is not true; the major bat companies on the market are experts at creating this illusion. The number one hoax pulled on the baseball community today is the illusion that the brand of bat makes the difference in performance. The expertise of today's marketing geniuses who offer appealing phrases, names, and conjured-up details of certain bats in an effort to differentiate themselves from the competitors in the market is indeed very clever.

Having the notion that you look good on the field makes you feel like an all-star. Feeling good on the diamond is definitely a plus for confidence and mental psyche. Sometimes, these illusionary factors can be used to benefit a player's game. If a parent has the resources to pacify a child's need to be "cool" and go for the pricier bat out of the selection at your local sporting goods store, by all means go for it. However, if you are a parent looking to be more economical, don't panic. There is no need to feel as if you are somehow doing your child a disservice by choosing a lesser known-brand bat.

Depending on the age of the player, it is very likely they will outgrow the bat after one season. Whether it is growing taller and needing a longer length, change of league regulations, or new certification requirements, the bat could only be needed for one or two years. There are probably many decent and barely used baseball bats piling up in your garage at this very moment. There also exists the inconvenience of not being able to sell them off as "used" when they are no longer needed. Veteran baseball parents are fully aware of this all too common problem.

There are basically two options when choosing a bat:
- The one that will satisfy the mental psyche of the player (aka "The Cool Bat").
- The bat that is more economically priced and affordable (aka" The Cheaper Bat that Saves us Money but Still Gets Results").

Now, you may be thinking to yourself, "But are there *any* differences in bats at all?" The answer is yes. There are a few subtle differences in a bat that may differentiate itself from the rest. Here are a few:

Weight Distribution - Some bats are more evenly distributed throughout from top to bottom. Some may be more "top heavy" or "handle heavy," meaning the bat feels heavier at one end or the other. This may make a small difference in how it initially feels, but with proper technique it should not make a large difference.

Bat Handle Grip - The grip of the bat is also part of the "comfortability" factor when talking about what *feels* good. This is one factor that I would personally consider a legitimate preference to have because you want the bat to feel comfortable in your hands. Some bat grips are softer while others are more firm. You don't always have to stick with the grip that came with the bat. Different grips can be bought and switched out as desired, which is why I wouldn't recommend purchasing a bat based off of grip preference alone.

But, wait...wouldn't bats ranging in different types of metal make a difference? You mean to tell me that titanium, composite, or aluminum bats don't differ or vary in performance?

To this I'd say that giving too much attention to these types of things would be misdirecting our focus on more important areas. For years and years there has been inconclusive evidence on whether or not one type of metal excels over another. There has been scientific research and studies done to put a rest to this debate and

111

different conclusions have been made. A multitude of characteristics of bats are examined, including trampoline effect, bending stiffness, bending vibration, and many others.

To rely on a bat to deliver the performance we desire would definitely contribute to us "missing the point" about what is important. Putting too much stock in which type of bat is what would only strengthen the aforementioned *illusion* as described earlier.

In my freshman year of college, I had no idea what to expect at the next level. Since I had success with the brand of bat that I used throughout my high school career, I figured, "Hey, if it isn't broken, don't fix it!" and decided I would continue with the same brand at my new college. When I got to my first practice, all of the upperclassmen had the same bat as one another. There was only one thing that confused me, though: It wasn't the same brand I had.

After being kindly interrogated by an inquisitive upperclassman about my bat, it was then explained to me that we were sponsored by another well-known brand and that at the start of the season I would be obligated to use that particular brand in all games. But what if I wasn't comfortable with this new brand that I was forced to use? What if I thought that the brand I was used to hitting withheld a significant advantage over this other bat that I was now expected to use? This was the start of the realization that good hitters can hit with any brand and any type of bat.

From a recruiting perspective for older players, college recruiters don't go to games to scout players and focus in on the brand of equipment that is being used. You'd be hard pressed to find a scout say "Ya know… I really like that player. I think he's strong, got quick hands and good mechanics. But I'm not really too interested in signing him because he uses an Easton bat and I doubt he'd be able to swing a Nike bat, which we're sponsored by. I think I'll pass."

Mechanics, Mechanics, Mechanics!

Height, weight, and strength level are all important factors when determining what bat size should be purchased or used. Although these are relative factors to utilize, they are not always absolute determinants. What size is best for swinging for your child may vary due to player preference. In Major League Baseball, all lengths and sizes are used by a wide range of players with a variance in physical make-up. For example, home-run hitter Barry Bonds not only used a relatively shorter bat than most players but also choked up on his bat during games to give himself more bat control while swinging.

Bat Control

The main and most important point of concern for any ball player as it pertains to a bat is **bat control.** What this means is that the player has full control of where the bat is directed during the swinging motion. A bat that is either too heavy or too long may cause the swing to be uncontrollable, which can make a player feel overwhelmed at the plate while batting. This will throw off timing and also cause a visible "struggle" in the swing that you should readily be able to notice during plate appearances (hitting during games).

I once had a player who had some technique problems with his swing. Without any recommendation, his father decided that he would go out and buy a brand new bat of a different size, feeling it that it would help with the mistakes. Low and behold, the player came back for more training after the brand new purchase. Unfortunately, he had the *same* mechanical issues as before. This goes to show that bad technique—not the bat size—could be the beginning of the problem. Though the wrong bat size could affect mechanics, ninety percent of the time, the first priority will be to get the right *type* of swing technique-wise.

If you feel like your child struggles with their swing, encourage them to choke up on the bat a couple of inches to enhance bat control. This will help determine if the issue is bat size or technique. If the issues do not subside after choking up, this will indicate that a bat size is too heavy or too long.

Here is a suggested guideline for bat size based off of player age, height, and weight:

Height	3'-3'4"	3'5"-3'8"	3'9"-4'	4'1"-4'4"	4'5"-4'8"	4'9"-5'	5'1"-5'4"	5'5"-5'8"	5'9"-6'
Weight									
< 60	26"	27"	28"	29"	29"				
61-70	27"	27"	28"	29"	30"	30"			
71-80		28"	28"	29"	30"	30"	31"		
81-90		28"	29"	29"	30"	30"	31"	32"	
91-100		28"	29"	30"	30"	31"	31"	32"	
101-110		29"	29"	30"	30"	31"	31"	32"	
111-120		29"	29"	30"	30"	31"	31"	32"	
121-130		29"	30"	30"	30"	31"	32"	33"	33"
131-140		29"	30"	30"	31"	31"	32"	33"	33"
141-150			30"	30"	31"	31"	32"	33"	33"
151-160			30"	31"	31"	32"	32"	33"	33"
161-180				31"	31"	32"	32"	33"	33"
181-190						32"	33"	33"	34"
190 +							33"	33"	34"

AGE	5-7	8-9	10	11-12	13-14	15-16
LENGTH	24"-26"	26"-28"	28"-29"	30"-31"	31"-32"	32"-33"

Aluminumbats.com

Keep in mind that these are just general suggestions. However, this will give you a good idea of where to start if you are unsure as to what size would be the right fit for your child.

Wooden bats

Since most players in the world of amateur baseball use regulated metal bats during gameplay, wooden bats are rarely ever used for practice or game purposes. Wooden bats are definitely worth the investment. Even if they are not required for gameplay in your current league or association, they are a great tool for any baseball player who has the intent of meaningful development.

Why is practicing with a wooden bat helpful?

The wooden bat offers a smaller "sweet spot" than the typical bat made out of metal. The sweet spot is the thickest part of the barrel and most ideal place to hit the ball. It provides the most power and hits the ball the greatest distance. When hitting with a wooden bat you are, in a way, forced to square the ball up on the smaller sweet spot if you want a desired result.

More choices are offered with wooden bats than metal. For beginners, different types include those made of ash, bamboo, hickory, and maple. Some players even choose the composite wooden bats. These are generally only used for practice purposes only. Wood composite is made of material that mocks wood and

115

offers a similar feel to real wood. They are far more durable than a real wooden bat and they are very hard to break, which is why composite is best if it is used only for practice.

Utilizing a wooden bat during practice time will make swinging metal bats during game time a piece of cake.

What if my child doesn't want to use the wooden bat for practice?

Many players initially struggle with the wooden bat, since it tends to expose their weaknesses. Remind them of its importance in helping them become better with the metal bat. Explain that it is going to be a different experience from a metal bat. It is important they know that they will not get the same results that they get with the metal bat (power or distance). Also, it doesn't hurt to remind them that the best of the best use it as well (MLB players).

"Whoever wants to know the heart and mind of America had better learn baseball."

-Jacques Barzun

17

Game Day Anxiety

Some individuals are born with the steel nerves that allow them to have zero worry, fear, or anxiety during an event, or in this case, a baseball game. Nervousness of this kind stems from the same reasons why a person is anxious about a big event they are scheduled to have, an important interview, or a major test: a fear of the unknown or a fear of a particular outcome that may occur.

The concept of fear is commonly explained in the acronym:

F-False

E-Evidence

A-Appearing

R-Real

This is the perfect acronym to describe this situation. Many things that players worry about before a game either do not end up happening or are false presumptions that are based off of faulty thinking patterns. In other words, I may be worried that I will fail, let my team down, and provoke the coach to yell at me in front of everyone, leaving me embarrassed. Not to say that this circumstance could not come about, but the chances of this happening are slim.

Reassurance is needed at times for all ball players, *especially* younger players. They need to know that how they feel is natural and something with which one can cope.

Parents can alleviate pre-game stress by telling their children they will be proud regardless of outcome. Many parents say, "Of course I'm proud of my son!" However, this is rarely vocalized. How else are they to know if you don't make it known through words? As a former youth player myself, I can attest that more times than not, the encouragement from my parent during an emotionally stressful time was always more important than that of any coach or teammate.

Other than emotional support, here are some in-game tips that may be useful:

Taking deep breaths - Deep breathing releases tension, relaxes the body, and brings mental clarity. You can do your part by encouraging deep breaths in between pitches during a game.

One pitch at a time - Oftentimes baseball players overwhelm themselves by trying to do too much at once. They must be reminded that baseball, like anything else in life, requires you to focus on one thing at a time.

There is a phrase that is often used in the higher ranks of baseball that perfectly sums up how every player should approach the game: "Win every pitch." This is a simple motto that encourages players to stay in the moment and to focus on the task at hand. The motto "Win every pitch" simply means each pitch or play has a life of its own that is independent of any previous plays that have already happened or any future plays that will happen. Well-known college football head coach Nick Saban is famous for his coaching style that mirrors this same philosophy. He and others like to label it as "The Process." This ideology is about focusing on the process of winning as opposed to the final outcome. Coach Saban has described "The Process" as a way to get his players to relieve anxiety and tension. He gets his players to buy into the idea that if each player focuses on his specific job during each and every play and performs to the best of his ability in that moment, the wins will take care of themselves.

Physical preparation - Arrive to the park earlier than usual so that you can allow for a thorough warm-up and stretching time. This will make the player feel more prepared to take on what is ahead of him.

Encourage to encourage - Inspire him to cheer his teammates on during a game. This will help divert his mind away from any negative thoughts about his performance and get him focused on *positivity*. It is difficult to *not* think positively when you are speaking such positive thoughts to others.

Most importantly, don't let *your* frantic obsession with their success interfere with *their* opportunities to have fun. Do not add onto what already may be an anxious moment for them. Believing in your child will help them begin believing in themselves. As a parent, when you sense your child may be nervous, talk about the success you envision them having in the upcoming game. This lets them know that you foresee them doing well and will spark a sense of assurance that will rid them of some—if not all—of their anxiety. If your child is willing to open up verbally about any anxious feelings, listen closely without judgment and see if you notice any particular patterns. If you backtrack and see exactly *why* a player is nervous or worried about a game, it can point you to the problem.

Nervousness and anxiety is a natural reaction. Sometimes experiencing these feelings multiple times is the *only* way an individual can move past it before they get to the point where it doesn't consume or prohibit them from performing as usual. In a lot of cases, it's just an emotional issue they will have to deal with for a while on their journey as a baseball player.

To recap, there are three main points that parents should remember and act on when dealing with a nervous player:

1. Show compassion and let them know that you understand how they are feeling.
2. Remind them of their previous successes.
3. Express that regardless of the outcome of the game, they will still be loved and appreciated.

"A baseball game is simply a nervous breakdown divided into nine innings."

-Earl Wilson

18

Pregame Nutrition: What and What Not to Eat

When it comes to performance improvement, ballplayers tend to put nutrition behind weight training, running, icing, and stretching. Paying attention to what goes in your body as an athlete will automatically set you apart from the majority of athletes, who sometimes don't give nutrition a second thought.

More than likely a youth baseball player will not follow a diet as strict as an Olympic athlete; however, giving more attention to diet than in the past can be beneficial.

Sodas, candy bars, oily potato chips, and cupcakes are some of the foods and beverages that are often consumed hours—even minutes—before a baseball game or practice. Players and parents are often forgetful of the importance of a healthy meal before going out to play a baseball game. The meal consumed before a game is vital for optimal energy and is important to eliminate the sluggishness that might hinder a player from performing at his highest abilities.

The best foods and drinks to intake before a game are those that will keep the blood sugar level at its highest, which will give longer-lasting energy. It is best to eat a combination of carbohydrates, lean protein, fruits, vegetables, and healthy fats one to three hours before game time to allow complete digestion.

Here are some simple meal ideas to keep a player's energy level at its highest for the duration of a game:

Do's — Breakfast	Don'ts — Breakfast
• Bagels • Yogurt • Bananas, apples & other fruits • Whole grain cereal	• Pork/ Beef sausage • Bacon • Fast food breakfast • Cereal with high sugar content
Do's — Lunch/Dinner	**Don'ts — Lunch/Dinner**
• Whole grain pasta (spaghetti or fettuccine) • Lean meats • Peanut butter & jelly sandwich • Bananas, apples & other fruits	• Beef or pork • Dairy with high fat content • Greasy or fried substances • FAST FOOD!

If you are on the road and find yourself limited in food options, don't think that you are stuck having to purchase fast food. Stop by the nearest grocery store and get a sandwich from the deli section if you were not able to pack your own healthy lunch or dinner. This is significantly better than choosing greasy fast food.

Consummation of a particular beverage *during* a game to stay hydrated is *just* as important as what a player eats before a game. One of the most important points one must remember is that hydration starts *before* the game. Properly hydrating the body prior to game time prevents the need to overload the body with fluids during the game, which may cause discomfort and abdominal cramps.

Stay away from soda at all costs before a game. Soda can be a major reason for the dehydration of an athlete due to its caffeinated, carbonated, and high sugar content. Most are fans of the popular sports drinks and juices that are on the market today; however, most of these drinks are very high in sugar.

Water should be on the top of the list when it comes to hydrating before, during, and after a game. On average, water makes up sixty to seventy percent of body weight and plays a very important role in helping transport nutrients and oxygen to the muscle cells and other tissue cells of the body. It is vital that water is consumed regularly, since intense exercise and physical exertion causes body fluids (mainly water) to secrete in order to prevent the body from rising to high temperatures.

The body's thirst mechanism has a "lag time" that triggers *after* the body reaches a point of dehydration. This is why it is very important to hydrate consistently regardless of feeling thirsty or not. This is why once you realize you're thirsty, you're more than likely already dehydrated. I've seen players pass out—or come close to it— from dehydration or exhaustion from not getting the proper nutrition.

Many times, when I ask players what they have eaten before a training session, I get off-the-wall responses that baffle me. Sometimes my conversations with young ball players will go in this manner:

> **Me:** *Are you tired today? You seem a bit sluggish. What did you eat before you came?*
>
> **Player:** *A pork chop sandwich that my mom made for lunch.*
>
> **Me:** *Hmmm, okay. What did you have to drink with it?*
>
> **Player:** *A cherry cola soda.*

This happens far more times than it should and it has become the norm, unfortunately. The absolute worst conversations I have with a player about his eating habits go as follows:

> **Me:** *Are you excited and ready to train this morning?*
>
> **Player:** *Yes…*
>
> **Me:** *What did we have for breakfast today?*
>
> **Player:** *Ummm…I didn't…have anything.*

The fact that a player chose to skip out on breakfast is indicative of nutritional expectation in the household, starting with the parents. Parents must have firm expectations when it comes to what is or what isn't being allowed for consumption prior to practices or games. Giving the responsibility to the child of what they should eat will normally end with an unhealthy choice.

With the access to information that is available in today's world, it is much easier to be informed about how nutrition can help players become better athletes.

"*The difference in winning or losing is most often not quitting.*"

-Walt Disney

19

Recreational League Baseball vs. Travel Baseball

The majority of youth baseball is played within the local community recreational parks across America. More and more parents are signing their sons up for travel baseball. There are even variations of travel baseball that are confined to local "travel" leagues, where teams play travel ball caliber competition within a localized proximity.

Most parents know the general differences that recreational league ("rec ball") play and travel ball play have on a basic level, but some still wonder what underlying differences there are between the two.

Here are a few of the major differences between recreational league and travel baseball.

Price

There is a stark difference between the two options when it comes to financial obligations. Recreational league is generally cheaper due to the fact that rec ball leagues have a relatively basic league structure. Since the majority of community parks are funded by tax payer dollars, there is less of a burden on those who join these leagues. Majority of cost is upfront and go to uniforms, bats, cleats, and general league fees that are fairly low.

Travel baseball is much more of a financial investment. The keyword in travel baseball is "travel," which automatically means that gas, hotel, and eating out have to be accounted for. Aside from travel expenses, upfront cost is a major factor. Tournament costs are a substantial portion of a travel teams expenses.

The prices to enter into prestigious tournaments could be hundreds of dollars per team. Since it is not unusual for a travel team to play multiple games in a week or even one day, uniform costs are double that of the rec ball costs for uniforms (some travel teams may have three to four different uniforms that are alternated throughout the season).

Time Commitment

Time commitment is a major difference. With rec ball, the schedule usually does not change and parents know *exactly* when and where games will be held (unless in the case of a rescheduled game due to rain out, etc.). Practices for recreational leagues are normally held once or twice a week at best. Since multiple rec teams use the same fields, this will limit the time that one team spends on the field for practice, as other teams are in line to use the next available slots. This could mean that rec ball parents normally only have to block off a two-hour window during the week for practice.

Travel baseball's time commitments may be four or five times that of the rec ball time commitment. Since the competition level is higher, coaches for travel ball teams schedule more practices during preseason and while the season is in full swing. Travel league tournaments could last anywhere from a couple of days to a whole week. Since tournament playing times are based on wins and losses, it is difficult to pinpoint what exact time a player's games will take place.

This could mean that your whole weekend is spent at a baseball park. For example, a player's loss at a tournament at 10:00 a.m. means they will play another game the same day at 3:00 p.m. If the team had won the game in the morning, it is possible they would not have played the second game until 5:00 p.m. This is just one example of how time can be stretched out in travel baseball tournaments.

Competition Level

The biggest visible different between a rec ball game and a travel league game is the level of competition on the field. Although there are good players who decide to join rec leagues, you are more likely to find more skilled players on travel league teams. Travel league players are not always more talented, but with a larger amount of time spent focused on the game due to more practices and games, players usually take the game more seriously (sometimes by default).

If a player is the top player on his rec ball team by a substantial amount, he should definitely consider stepping up to travel league to prevent complacency. It is always a good idea

133

to play against competition that is slightly better in order to improve.

Tryout Format

How tryouts work for recreational leagues is substantially different from the tryout format in travel baseball. In a recreational league, you are guaranteed a spot within a team. Signing up means a player automatically has a slot on a team. Coaches are assigned players usually based off of a draft style of choosing individuals in order to make teams as evenly matched in talent as possible.

For travel baseball, things are much different. For the most part, anything goes when it comes to team selection. Most travels teams are independent from a park or league. Coaches for travel baseball have no regulations on how they pick up particular players to join their teams. For the most part, age is the only regulated factor.

Players are chosen for multiple reasons, including player talent level, player attitude, parent attitudes, player loyalty, or sponsorship purposes. Group or private tryouts could be held at any time of the year for travel ball, unlike rec ball. Travel ball tryout competition is usually stiff because new, incoming players are competing with players who were on that particular travel team the year before. This may leave only a select amount of spots available.

Team Politics

We all would agree that both travel baseball teams and recreational baseball teams have their fair share of politics.

Regardless of sport, what's known as "daddy ball" is prevalent at the youth level. Every parent has suspected a coach or number of coaches participating in this common practice. Since youth leagues do not have the resources to hire full-time coaches, they usually rely on dads who are willing to volunteer their free time to serve as the designated team coaches.

Although team politics may be difficult to escape for either travel or recreational league, the dynamic is less prevalent in travel ball because the competition level is greater, leaving less and less room for nepotism. The focus tends to be more on winning games.

These are some major deciding factors that determine whether or not your child should play in a recreational league or on a travel ball team:

1. Player's current talent level
2. Family schedule and prior commitments that will affect availability
3. How serious the player and parents are about the player's future in the game of baseball
4. Financial flexibility

If your child plays on the rec level, there is no need to be discouraged if he has a desire to play on a higher level. I did not play on my first travel ball team until I was twelve years old, which may be considered late by some within the baseball community. Whether it is rec ball or travel ball, personal player development should be top priority.

"Playing baseball is not real life. It's a fantasy world—it's a dream come true."

-Dale Murphy

20

How to Deal with Injuries

Having a child who is playing with an injury could be tricky business, for the simple fact that you can't feel their level of discomfort or pain. Are they *too* injured to participate in games or practice? Are they exaggerating on their level of pain? Though you can tell if your child is injured by visually seeing swelling, bruising, or limping, there are some injuries that take place that are not as easy to readily spot. When an injury *does* occur, taking precautionary action is vital to the health and future performance of the child.

As much as some parents would like to say "Suck it up! Get out there and play!" or "You're just being a cry baby. You'll be fine, keep playing!" it is important to be tactful. However, do not set a standard that would allow your son to throw in the towel after every scrape and scratch.

Unless there is a noticeable injury, the right questions will need to be asked in order to know what action steps to take.

1. What does it feel like?

This sounds vague and general, but this will give the player an opportunity to say what is on his mind free from influence of what he *thinks* he needs to say. If a child is being asked about an injury while already aware of the fact that the parent doesn't believe the injury is bad, they may feel as if they have to lie about the intensity of the injury to appease the parent, which could make things worse.

2. How long has it been hurting?

This will give insight on whether this was a gradual or an acute injury. Gradual injuries are caused from continuous activity that leads to a gradual breakdown of muscle tissue or gradual buildup of inflammation in a joint. It is possible that the player has been playing through an injury for an extended amount of time but was scared to speak up about it to the parent. This is why it is not recommended to be highly judgmental towards a player who reports injury. It only takes one time to be scolded for reporting an injury to cause a player to feel that they have to keep all other injuries to themselves. This could cause even more damage.

3. Is the pain too much to play with?

This will give you the most accurate second-hand understanding of the level of pain the player is experiencing. If a player claims that his injury is too much to continue to play with, take heed to those claims and consider seeing a doctor for further review. Playing with discomfort and playing through actual *pain* are two different matters. A scrape or a bruise may involve just toughing up, but if you see that a player cannot bear weight on his lower extremities or make certain movements in particular body parts, it is time to make some serious considerations.

Throwing Shoulder Injuries

The most common injury in baseball is to the throwing arm shoulder. With the mechanics in which a baseball is thrown, which is often deemed an "unnatural motion," many players experience a time in their careers when they go through a shoulder injury. This injury is hard to avoid, since all positions on the field deal with the over-the-top throwing motion. It is part of the game, and if a player plays long enough, he will experience at least a mild discomfort at some point while throwing. Paying attention to what types of pains a player feels is important.

Sharp Pains vs. Dull Pains

A sharp pain is mostly indicative of a more acute injury, usually involving trauma to the joint area (shoulder or elbow). Elbow injuries tend to stem from poor mechanics while throwing. Poor mechanics can consist of incorrect arm motion or insufficient use of the legs during the throw, which help generate power to take pressure off of the arm. This is what those in the baseball community refer to as "using all arm."

Without the torque needed using the upper body/core along with pushing off of the back leg to propel the body towards its target, you not only increase chances of injury but you also lose velocity on throws. Unfortunately, most players do not learn the proper way to throw, which leads to an early breaking down of the arm. Year after year, the baseball community sees younger and younger players opting to get surgery to repair damaged shoulders and elbows. Younger and weaker arms cannot afford the wrong mechanics.

Players who are further along in skill are usually called upon to throw more pitches—these types of players are usually the ones whose arm may break down faster. Parents must establish a firm understanding with coaches about pitch count (number of pitches a pitcher is allowed to throw per game). Coaches can be so focused on winning games that the player's safety is placed on the back burner. Important tournament games, playoff games, and championship games cause youth league players to stretch beyond their physical capabilities to deliver for their team.

Although it's very understandable to "ride the horse," (a player who figuratively carries his team on his back) usually no real thought is given to that player's well-being in the *future*. Like I mentioned before, to a degree this is understandable because we can all get caught up in the moment. However, that is why it is even more essential that boundaries and guidelines be set in place *before* the game situation gets too deep. It is in the best interest of the parents—and the players—to set forth a *firm* pitch count. Your team may not have an official pitch count for every player, but that would be no excuse for *you* not to demand one for *your* child.

Here is a list of suggested pitch count and resting time in between games that should be required for all age groups:

Age	Pitches/Game
7-8	50
9-10	75
11-12	85
13-16	95
17-18	105

Maximum Pitch Counts

Ages 14 and under	Ages 15–18	Required # of Rest Pitches
66+	76+	4 calendar days
51–65	61–75	3 calendar days
36–50	46–60	2 calendar days
21–35	31–45	1 calendar day
1-20	1–30	None

Source: Little League Baseball

Age Recommended for Various Pitches

Pitch	Age
Fastball	8±2
Slider	16±2
Change-up	10±3
Forkball	16±2
Curveball	14±2
Knuckleball	15±3
Screwball	17±2

Source: From work by James R. Andrews, MD, and Glenn S. Fleisig, PhD

These throwing shoulder injuries can happen for players at any position, which they usually do. Similar steps can be taken to help heal pain.

Players at higher ranks of baseball have used long distance

running as a means of helping with shoulder muscle/joint pain. This helps flush the buildup of lactic acid in or around the muscles and joints from all of the strenuous activity. This is why high school, college, and professional players who are experiencing arm pain are usually seen running around a track or doing sprints from foul pole to foul pole on the baseball field immediately after they finish pitching a game. This allows lactic acid to be flushed out of the areas of pain and prevents the acid from accumulating and settling in the affected areas (joints, tendons, muscles). This remedy is not often used amongst the youth age level, but it holds just as much benefit.

Icing the affected area of the throwing arm is a well-known tactic for combating pain. Ice plays an intricate part in helping with inflammation. Ice can be used after games or during off days when a player isn't being active. Never use ice on the arm before a game, as it will be counteractive when trying to warm-up in pre-game preparations.

Although the shoulder is the most commonly injured area for baseball players, your son may experience anything from a twisted ankle to a sprained knee. In this case, a common recipe for injury of all sorts has been the *"R.I.C.E"* remedy.

- **Rest -** Proper rest and refrain from unnecessary physical activity that may aggravate an injury gives the cells time to regenerate and rebuild in the affected areas.
- **Ice -** Applying ice on and off for fifteen to twenty minutes at a time promotes an anti-inflammatory effect.
- **Compression -** Excessive swelling can hinder blood flow. Compression can come in the form of a bandage or a stocking.

142

- **Elevation** - (normally for lower extremities, i.e. ankles, feet, knee) helps with blood flow and circulation.

Most would agree that taking it a step further and using *"P.R.I.C.E"* may be a more suitable acronym to live by. (P is for *PREVENTION*)

Pre-habilitation (pre-hab)

If there is nothing else you learn about baseball injuries, especially the throwing arm, it's ***"pre-habilitation is better than rehabilitation."*** Pre-hab consists of all steps taken with the objective of *preventing* an injury before it happens. Of course, not all can be considered preventable, but at least we can do what is necessary to lessen our chances of ending up on the Disabled List (DL). With the throwing arm (shoulder/elbow), as mentioned before, being the main focus of rehab for a lot of baseball injuries, it goes without saying that majority of focus for pre-hab would involve precautionary measures for the arm.

Arm Band Exercises

A good athletic band program will help strengthen the arm, allowing the surrounding muscles to give the much-needed support the elbow and shoulder joints need while throwing. This is a great source of at-home exercise that every baseball player should partake in to prevent injury. Once again, this should be done regardless of whether a player is currently experiencing injury or not.

In fact, a *stronger* throwing arm is usually a byproduct of pre-hab, not just the prevention of injury. Athletic bands can be found at any local sporting goods store, but are more easily found at baseball specific stores (or online stores). Plenty of examples of how to perform various arm band exercises can be found through the internet or in online videos.

Remedy and prevention for body aches, soreness and stiffness

Athletic activities yield wear and tear on the body. At times a player will experience stiffness and soreness in places they wouldn't have expected. Double headers and back-to-back game days will push a player's body to the limit. Learning to take care of the body should be learned early on in a baseball career—just like learning to maintain the upkeep of an automobile should be the focus of any new car owner.

Using sea salt soaks is a very therapeutic yet underused tool for the removal of accumulated lactic acid in the body. As mentioned before, when the body performs strenuous workouts and physical activities, lactic acid can build up in the muscle tissues, which contributes to an individual feeling stiff and sore. When soaking, the salt water penetrates the pores and is then absorbed into the bloodstream. This is where the removal of lactic acid build up takes place due to the alkalizing effect of the sea salt. Be sure that sea salt—not common table salt—is used. Some of the most recommended variations of sea salt include:

- Celtic
- Himalayan
- French
- Atlantic

Run warm to hot water in a bathtub while adding about sixteen ounces of sea salt to the water. This method is excellent for pre-hab or rehab.

The body is the biggest tangible asset a player has, so it must be taken care of. Parents hold the key to instilling this into their young ball player's minds early in their playing careers. Acquiring the proper knowledge and doing the research to find out how to combat injury will keep players on the field much longer with increased performance.

"A person always doing his or her best becomes a natural leader, just by example."

-Joe DiMaggio

21

The Three-Step System

A side from more detailed advice, like what has been shared thus far within the previous chapters, I want to conclude with a very simple three-step system to encompass all that has been discussed. As parents, this system is an effective way to teach younger players how to break down the process of achieving a high goal without overwhelming themselves. Anyone looking to capitalize on their potential can use these three steps to transform into a better player:

Change of Mindset

"Thoughts, choices and actions must harmonize with desires."

The initial step in this process is to change the mindset. A change in actions must first start with a change in how one thinks. A player who wishes to reach new heights has to make sure that his thoughts are positive and only focused on achievement. From attitude, choice of words, body language, and overall demeanor, his mindset must reflect what he wants to see take place in physical reality.

Formulate a Plan of Action

"He who fails to plan, plans to fail." -Winston Churchill

After his mindset has changed for the better, he is then motivated to take action. With no real action plan, his efforts will not be utilized efficiently. The next step is to come up with a game plan for how he will make this transformation into the player he would like to become. This strategy can consist of a plan to go see a private instructor during certain days of the week, doing a regimen of at-home drills that will improve skill, or devising a workout plan to increase strength and conditioning.

For each one of my clients, I normally devise a plan that is specific to that particular player. This plan may involve drills or workouts that reflect what I feel the player needs to work on the most. Creating a spreadsheet with the days of the week and drills listed can be very useful. It serves as a means of holding players accountable. Here is an example of a spreadsheet with workouts and drills that I would create for a client:

At-home Development Plan	Mon	Tues	Wed	Thurs	Fri
Tee Drill 15 Reps x 3 Sets	✓	✓			
One-hand Tee Drill 15 Reps Each	✓	✓			
Pushups 20 x 4 Sets	✓	✓			
Stress Ball Hand Exercise 25 Reps x 4 sets	✓	✓			

The chart is used as a visual reminder to keep players on track while sticking to a regimen. I instruct my clients to check off each individual box as they have completed each segment. The goal is to have the entire chart filled with check marks by the end of the week. This visual serves as evidence that they have put in extra work, which will give them a sense of achievement. It can be the catalyst to becoming even more excited about the concept of diligence and hard work. If you aren't sure of what exercises or drills to add into the plan, you can always ask a trusted source or find a variety of ideas through videos on the internet.

Develop the Discipline to Stay on Path

"Men are anxious to improve their circumstances, but are unwilling to improve themselves; they therefore remain bound." - James Allen

After a change in mental state inspires us to make a plan to take action, we then face the challenges of sticking to it long enough to see results. Oftentimes, the initial stages of intense motivation for a player can deplete quickly. It takes true discipline to carry out a plan of action until the desired results appear. After all, this is the hardest phase within this three-step system. Everyone is quite aware of the "secret" to success in anything, which is preparation and hard work. This isn't a secret at all. The real secret the average person can't seem to solve is how to develop the discipline to stick with the plan of action that is required to succeed.

Here is an instance when a child has to exercise their discipline through the discipline of the parent. If a child knows that their parent is lacking the very discipline that they preach, the chances of them going through with a plan of action for long enough to see results is unlikely. To ensure that your player stays on track through an extended period of time, you must have the discipline to hold them accountable over a prolonged timeframe. Oftentimes, excitement and motivation towards a goal will fizzle out quickly with both the parent and the child. This is why this final step in the Three Step System is most difficult. Utilizing a visual chart like the example in the "Formulate a plan of action" phase may be the best way to exercise discipline. This provides an easy way to look back over a period of time and actually *see* that you have stuck to a plan.

"A ballplayer spends a good piece of his life gripping a baseball, and in the end it turns out that it was the other way around all the time."

- Jim Bouton

Final Thoughts

In closing, it is my hope that after reading the material presented in this book you have a better understanding on how you, as a parent, can contribute to developing a better and more refined baseball player. I hope that I have explained to you the false notion that you have to be a former Major League or semi-professional baseball player to make a substantial impact.

On this unpredictable road to success for a baseball player, it isn't just the player that is affected. As long as baseball has been an option for extracurricular activity, there have been parents who have strived to help in every possible way.

With the onset of new technology and equipment rapidly being introduced, the landscape of youth baseball has changed. The principles discussed here are timeless and could also be beneficial in other sports or endeavors in which your child may take an interest. I'm quite sure you will find it appropriate to share this information with other parents within the community who may be dealing with the similar duties of being a baseball parent.

"Baseball is a game of inches."

This old adage is use quite frequently to describe how subtle advantages can lead to exponential gains. The older players get, the more they will need to rely on these small advantages to separate themselves from the increasing competition. Having a Game Changer as a parent is the first step.

Author's Biography

Michael McCree, a former collegiate baseball player who received a 4-year scholarship at Georgia State University, has coached hundreds of youth baseball players through private and team training and continues to have a widespread impact on players and parents alike. He currently coaches in Atlanta, Georgia and other surrounding areas. With a Master's of Science degree in Sports Administration, his main focus in athletics is geared toward the development and achievement of youth athletics. His work is attributed to his strong belief that youth athletic involvement is an essential tool in the refinement of character.

Glossary

Base on Balls or BB ("Pregame Conversations") - is credited to a batter and against a pitcher in baseball statistics when a batter receives four pitches that the umpire calls balls. It is better known as a walk.*

Baseball IQ ("Why it's Important to Learn from the Best") - an intangible asset to a player that reflects his knowledge, ability to spot in-game situations, and his adaptability. Baseball IQ cannot be measured numerically.

Choke up ("The Truth about Bats") - gripping the hands closer to the barrel and further away from the nob of the bat. This is done usual to give the hitter more bat control.

Daddy Ball ("Recreational ball vs. Travel ball") - a coach who plays his child either in a preferred position or increased playing time, at the exclusion of other athletes who may be more talented.

Hit By Pitch or HBP ("Character Building in Baseball") - is a batter or his equipment (other than his bat) being hit by a pitch from the pitcher. A hit batsman is awarded first base, provided that (in the plate umpire's judgment) he made an honest effort to avoid the pitch.

*Source: Wikipedia

"Good outs" ("How to Handle Slumps") - an at-bat that results in helping the team or an out where a player produced a solid hit ball right at or near an opposing player. Good outs can also be described as "non-easy outs" or anything that forces the opposing team to give extra effort in order to get a player out.

Ground Ball ("Character Building in Baseball") - a ball hit by a player that results in the baseball rolling on the ground.

Line Drive ("How to handle slumps") - a type of batted ball that is sharply hit and on (or slightly above) a level trajectory.*

Plate Appearance ("How to Handle Slumps") - Every trip by a batter to the plate, including hits, walks, outs and reach by error. (Baseball-reference.com)

Platoon Player ("Finding a Role on the Team") - a method of designating two players to a single defensive position—usually one right-handed and one left-handed. Typically the right-handed half of the platoon is played on days when the opposing pitcher is left-handed and the left-handed player is played otherwise. The theory behind this is that generally players hit better against their opposite-handed counterparts, and that in some cases the difference is extreme enough to warrant complementing the player with one of opposite-handedness.*

Pinch Hitter ("Finding a Role on the Team") - a substitute batter.

*Source: Wikipedia

"Prehabilitation" ("Dealing with Injury") - all actions and precautionary steps taken with the objective of preventing an injury before it happens.

Sacrifice Bunt (also called a sacrifice hit) ("How to Handle Slumps" and "Finding a Role on the Team") - a batter's act of deliberately bunting the ball, before there are two outs, in a manner that allows a runner on base to advance to another base. The batter is almost always sacrificed (and to a certain degree that is the intent of the batter) but sometimes reaches base due to an error or fielder's choice.*

Sacrifice Pop Fly ("Character Building in Baseball") - a batted ball that satisfies four criteria:

1. There are fewer than two outs when the ball is hit.
2. The ball is hit to the outfield (fair or foul), or to infield foul territory.
3. The batter is put out because an outfielder (or an infielder running in the outfield, or foul territory) catches the ball on the fly (alternatively if the batter would have been out if not for an error or if the outfielder drops the ball and another runner is put out).
4. A runner who is already on base scores on the play.

It is called a "sacrifice" fly because the batter presumably intends to cause a teammate to score a run, while sacrificing his own ability to do so.*

Source: Wikipedia

Switch Hitter ("Being a Versatile Player) - a player who bats both right-handed and left-handed—right-handed against left-handed pitchers, and left-handed against right-handed pitchers.

Slump ("How to handle a Slump") - a period when player or team is not performing well or up to expectations.

Spot Duty ("Finding a Role on the Team") - when a player is called upon to execute a specific game plan. Many within the baseball community label as being called to "do a job." Spot duties may consist of substituting into a game for the purpose of:

- Bunting to move a runner over
- Pinch hitting
- Entering a game as a pitcher during a situation that offers a good pitcher-hitter matchup
- Entering as a substitute at the end of a close game for defensive purposes

References

Abraham, Esther Hicks, and Jerry Hicks. *The Law of Attraction: The Basics of the Teachings of Abraham.* Carlsbad, CA: Hay House, 2006. Print. AbrahamHicks.com, (830) 755-2299

Little League Baseball. www.littleleague.org/Assets/old_assets/media/pitchcount_faq_08.pdf

Prevention and Emergency Management of Youth Baseball and Softball Injuries. American Orthopaedic Society for Sports Medicine. 2005.

Rusczyk, R. Art of Problem Solving Incorporated. Learning Through Teaching. Retrieved November, 2013 from http://www.artofproblemsolving.com/Resources/

Schreiber, LeAnne. "This is Your Brain On Sports." *Science Behind Watching the Game.* (2011): n. page. Web. 25 Nov. 2013. http://www.grantland.com/story/_/id/7179471/this-your-brain-sports.

Wegner, Daniel M. *White Bears and Other Unwanted Thoughts: Suppression, Obsession, and the Psychology of Mental Control.* New York, NY: Viking, 1989. Copyright Guilford Press. Reprinted with permission of The Guilford Press